"I have taught Healing Touch for over 30 year and Judy's book does an exceptional job of weaving together the significant qualities and energies of each of the chakras, along with meditations and visualizations to support each of the different energies of the chakras ... Judy's book is truly an excellent guide to activating one's Inner Healer and finding deep peace."

Anne L. Day, BSN, MA, HNB-BC, CHTP/I, and Journaling Instructor. thehealingjourneys.com

"This book is a gift for your spirit. I found it to be incredibly rich – filled with wonderful stories, anecdotes and perspectives, with poems and quotations woven throughout, all tied together in a stunningly beautiful way. I am grateful to have this book as a resource and a gift in Judy's voice, that I will turn to time and time again."

Carolyn Maue, Leadership Development Coach, President, The Maue Center, Author, *Gourmet Leadership: Turn up the heat on your secret sauce!*

"The simple but life changing "effortless effort" of relaxing the body, engaging with the breath and focusing the mind is an ancient practice, passed down and honed by many traditions. In Finding Peace ... [this is] especially resonant with the contemporary heart, offering peace and inner strength in an often overwhelming but always beautiful and endlessly interconnected universe."

Stephanie Malleus, MD, FAAFP

"Through her inspired meditations, beautiful stories and clear explanations of chakras and energy fields, Judy has written an instructional manual for finding peace ... This is not a book to be read once and put away ... As you face new challenges and circumstances in your daily life, you will want to go back and find the right meditation or story to ground you and guide you as you move forward."

Barbara H. Stratton, Esq.

Finding Peace

**Meditations and Stories
for Insight and Balance**

Judith Lynch Stoddard

CKBooks Publishing

No part of this book may be reproduced, scanned, or distributed in any print or electronic form without the author's permission.
Contact the author at jlstod@aol.com.

Publisher's Cataloging-in-Publication Data
provided by Five Rainbows Cataloging Services

Names: Stoddard, Judith Lynch, author.
Title: Finding peace : meditations and stories for insight and balance / Judith Lynch Stoddard.
Description: New Glarus, WI : CKBooks Publishing, 2024. | Includes bibliographical references.
Identifiers: ISBN 978-0-9881993-4-7 (paperback) | ISBN 978-1-966219-09-5 (ebook)
Subjects: LCSH: Chakras--Health aspects. | Energy medicine. | Mental healing. | Motivation (Psychology) | Mind and body. | BISAC: BODY, MIND & SPIRIT / Healing / Energy (Chakras, Qigong, Reiki) | BODY, MIND & SPIRIT / Mindfulness & Meditation. | HEALTH & FITNESS / Healing.
Classification: LCC BF1442.C53 S76 2024 (print) | LCC BF1442.C53 (ebook) | DDC 155.9/37--dc23.

LCCN: 2024920445

Cover photo: blown glass from A Thin Place, Iona, Scotland.
Photo taken by Robert Stoddard
Author photo by Jon Ripsom Photography

Copyright © 2024 Judith Lynch Stoddard
All Rights Reserved

Published by CKBooks Publishing
PO Box 214
New Glarus, WI, 53574
ckbookpublishing.com

This book is dedicated to my
husband, Robert Stoddard,
daughter, Carrie Saathoff, and her husband, Shawn,
Son, Malcolm Stoddard, and his wife, Lisa,
grandchildren,
Evelyn and Baden Saathoff,
Ella and Ian Stoddard,
Anam Cara, Regina Pippidis,
ancestors, known and unknown

Table of Contents

Introduction 1
Intention 6
Energy/Vibrational Medicine 8
Chakra/Aura Image 11
First Chakra (Root Support) 13
    Earthing/Grounding Meditation 15
    The Mother Tree Meditation 17
    Ancestors Meditation 20
    Remembrance Meditation 22
    The Healing Energy of Children 24
    Home Meditation 26
    Leaving Home 28
    Body Scan Meditation 32
    Simplify Meditation 36
    Full Moon Meditation 39

Second Chakra (Sacral) 43
    The Five Senses Meditation 45
    Laughter Meditation 48
    Stories and Poker 50
    Sparkle Meditation 52
    Sparkling Personalites 55
    Ken 57
    A Spring Meadow Journey Meditation 60

Third Chakra (Solar Plexus) 65
    Luminescent Russanne 67
    Courage Meditation 70
    Energetic Sweeping Meditation 73
    Spider Spiritual Symbol Meditation 76
    Tuning In to Yourself Meditation 78

    Journey Into Wellness,
    An Opportunity for Self-Healing and Learning ...82
    Self-Created Affirmations Meditation 85
    Superpowers Meditation 87

Fourth Chakra (Heart) 91
    Butterfly Blessings Meditation 93
    Gift of the Day 96
    Gifts from the Heart 97
    Caring for the World's Children,
    Heartstrings and Energetic Cords Meditation 99
    My Mother Was Buried in a Cookie Jar 102
    Tibetan Prayer Flags Meditation 104
    Indra's Net/Web Meditation 106
    Passing Time Meditation 108
    Healing and Dying 110
    Silence of the Heart Meditation 112
    The Gift of Bruno 115
    I Want Blue! 118

Fifth Chakra (Throat) 121
    Words Matter Meditation 123
    Lunchbox Notes 126
    Insights on Waiting 127
    Sun Power Meditation 128
    Armadillo Lessons 131
    Journaling for Clarity 132
    All Shall Be Well Affirmations Meditation 134

Sixth Chakra (Brow; Third Eye) 137
    Floating Meditation 139
    Intuition Quotes 142
    Candle Gazing 144
    A Preparation for Meditation 144

Back to Basics: A Meditation Template 146
Spirit Wind Meditation 148
Thin Places Meditation 151

Seventh Chakra (Crown) 155
Light 157
Spaciousness Meditation 159
Ribbons of Grace and Light Meditation 161
Julian's Prayer Meditation 163
We Are All Healers Meditation 165
Gabriel, Strength of God Meditation 167
Adventure in Moving 169

Afterword 171
Glossary 173
Bibliography 179
Resources 182
Images 184
Acknowledgments 186
About the Author 189

My Peace

I pass my peace around and about 'cross hands of every hue;
I guess my peace is justa 'bout all I've got to give to you.

— Woody Guthrie, "Words"
Arlo Guthrie, Music

Introduction

I have been writing this book for a number of years. I just didn't know I was.

Throughout my long and varied career in traditional nursing I kept abreast of developments in complementary care modalities. After my official retirement from nursing, I realized I was not only missing the profession but the spiritual fulfillment I received from being a nurse. I did not want to be reemployed, so I began considering how I might otherwise be of service.

To maintain my registered nurse licensure, thirty educational contact hours of study are required every two years. To meet this requirement, I often chose a holistic therapy subject. As I began to review the courses I had used for license renewal, I recalled that the course on Healing Touch (HT) had been of great interest, but because I was raising a family and working, I didn't have the time and energy to pursue it further. Now I did. I reread the textbook, wanted to learn more about the specialty, located a Level One class in a nearby state and, with a friend, signed on. At the end of the weekend I felt strongly that much of my nursing career and my life experiences had been guiding me toward learning about energy medicine and holistic healing.

The word "heal" means to be made whole, different from the word "cure," which means to be freed from symptoms or disease. Healing Touch is a centuries old holistic energy therapy in which practitioners use their hands in a heart-centered and intentional way to effectively promote relaxation and healing by decreasing anxiety, tension, stress, and pain, thereby assisting the body's self-healing processes. It can help diminish the side effects of remedial interventions such as chemotherapy and surgery, and supports traditional medical care. HT uses the biofield (chakras, meridians, auras) to restore balance by holistically focusing on the whole person—physically, emotionally, mentally, and spiritually (PEMS).

The Healing Touch course in which I enrolled consisted of five levels, and because no classes were given in Delaware where I lived, I traveled to New Jersey for the first three classes, to Arizona for Level Four, and to Minnesota for Level Five, both held in remote mountain areas. To advance from Level Four to Level Five, a student was required to be mentored for a year, write a long and detailed case study on a client, experience ten different energy medicine modalities, read ten books on related subjects, write critiques of both modalities and books, and offer one hundred gratis healing touch sessions. I completed the work to become a practitioner within two years, submitted required course work to become certified shortly thereafter, and have fulfilled requisites for recertification every five years since then.

Immediately after the first class, I started a small Healing Touch practice in our home. As my skills, confidence, and learning grew, so did my practice. Some of my clients were diagnosed with life-threatening illnesses and were undergoing treatment or were under hospice care. Others came to relieve personal stress or physical pain. It was a gift to be able to provide Healing Touch for several clients throughout the dying and death processes.

Years later when we downsized and moved to a neighborhood out of the city, my practice began to decrease. Seeing clients in person for hands-on sessions during the Covid pandemic became impossible. I was able to do remote sessions with clients but could not take on anyone new, thus decreasing my client base further. Interestingly, however, my practice turned in a new and exciting direction.

~ Judith Stoddard ~

In the late fall of 2019, with a supportive committee of three, I designed and led a Women's Holistic Spiritual weekend retreat for twenty-seven participants. Interest was expressed in finding ways to sustain the strong relationship building that had begun and discussions continued about how that could be accomplished after the holiday season. With the Covid shutdown in early 2020 our creative ideas for women's programming were tabled. "Retreaters" Zoom meetings were born and have continued twice monthly since then, having morphed into a smaller and meaningful core support group of retreat women.

Six months later, while meditating, the idea of starting a women's meditation group popped into my head. The thought persisted. Listening to my Intuitive Inner Teacher, I emailed retreat attendees and other women I knew asking if they would be interested in joining such a group. Twenty-two responded that they wanted to be included, most having little or no experience in meditating or energy-related subjects. The Friends and Friends of Friends meditation group was formed. Quite a few members have never met in person. We meditate together via Zoom twice monthly, and happily the group continues to grow.

The self-guided meditations found in this book are original and are enhanced with supportive information, poems, blessings, quotes, and the prayers of others. I encourage you to add your favorite readings. Journaling thoughts, insights, and images that come to you during meditation will enrich your experience. The meditations can easily be used in groups.

Finding Peace is meant to be a resource for wholeness and healing, a book to turn to when a specific chakra's gifts are needed (Root: grounding; Sacral: creativity; Solar Plexus: courage and self-esteem; Heart: love, compassion, grief; Throat: communication; Brow: Intuition; Crown: divine connection). I recommend reading the book straight through at least once to become familiar with its offerings. The meditations are not timed; there is no right or wrong way to use them or place in which to experience them. They are designed for both beginning and practiced meditators, for individuals knowledgeable of the biofield and its role in holistic healing and self-care, as well as for readers new to the ideas. They are simply a means for readers to find a quiet place within themselves to receive and share whatever is gifted to them. Although there are many descriptive names for a Higher Power, I have chosen to use the word Spirit to represent it throughout the book.

To meditate in a seated position, I recommend finding an area without external distractions. Sit comfortably with a straight spine and shoulders, neck, and facial muscles relaxed. The chin should be tilted downward slightly. To ground yourself, place your feet flat on the floor, preferably without shoes, or if outside, on the earth. To read the meditations, hold the book gently or place it in your lap. If the book is propped, place your hands comfortably in your lap or on your thighs, elbows pointing slightly outward.

The meditations employ visualization, using your imagination to form visual pictures without external stimuli. It is seeing in your Mind's Eye (or hearing with the Mind's Ear). Research has shown that visualization uses the same brain areas that actual seeing does and plays a crucial role in our perception and understanding of the world around us. Visualizing is easy for some individuals and may be more challenging for others. To develop or increase visualization skills, it is suggested that a person try not to overthink, stay nonjudgemental, use all senses, remain relaxed and emotionally connected, and simply practice. Visualize with a sense of knowing and trust that you can do it.

The format for the meditations is the same throughout:
- Introductory paragraph
- Set the Intention
- Relaxation breaths (slowly breathing in through the nose and out through mouth, making the exhalation twice as long as the inhalation); breathe normally throughout
- Experience the self-guided meditation
- Give thanks
- Relaxation breaths
- End quotations

My journey into the realm of energy medicine and related subjects was the gateway to my spiritual and intellectual growth and expansion in ways I never could have imagined. Viewing my life and the world "energetically" as I now do has made all the difference.

I have read that poets occasionally refer to poems that practically write themselves as "found poems." Countless ideas for my meditations and stories have come unbidden and in that sense can be considered "found." I consider them "found blessings."

I hope you enjoy reading *Finding Peace* as much as I enjoy sharing it with you.

~ Judith Stoddard

Intention

Setting an Intention is different from setting a goal. When we set a goal, we are oriented to a future outcome and plan how we are going to get there. When we set an Intention, we simply "intend" the outcome and entrust the process to the Universe or whatever Higher Power resonates in our life. Setting an Intention is heart centered, created out of love and something we are asking to have happen. It may seem like saying a prayer or making a wish.

When I begin a Healing Touch Session, I ask aloud that healing light, energy, and love come into clients and for them to be healed in all the ways they need to be healed, knowing that to be healed means to be made whole. I ask for centering, balancing, grounding, and clearing, and address the requests an individual has stated such as pain or stress relief, relaxation, clarity for decision making for a personal problem, respite from grieving, courage to face medical treatment or diagnosis, or other challenges they are facing in their life. I end by giving thanks for our time together, for our client/practitioner relationship, for the person's gifts and blessings, and for healing for the person's Highest Good.

Each meditation in the book begins with an Intention, a positive statement of what I hope Spirit (Higher Power as used here) will bring to the reader. Some Intentions are for self-care and healing, for personal growth and exploration, while others are meant to strengthen connections and bonds with people in your life and to offer opportunities for sending healing thoughts and concerns into the world. All Intentions are to help become aware of any gifts received during this quiet time.

I feel that setting an Intention is a way of tapping into

the Universal Law of Attraction: like attracts like, an ancient philosophy that can be traced back to the first century, AD. The principle is that positive thoughts manifest positive outcomes, and negative thoughts manifest negative outcomes.

Intentions are not just for use during Healing Touch sessions or meditations. They can be incorporated into everyday life experiences. Keep Intentions realistic. Not everything that we intend may be given to us. Perhaps the Universe has a more interesting and wonderful plan in store than we could ever envision. Stay open to all possibilities.

Our Intention creates our reality.
—Wayne Dyer

Energy/Vibrational Medicine

The Human Energy Field (HEF) and Energy Therapy Modalities

There is evidence of energy healing in ancient cultures throughout the world, including among native Americans. Eastern traditions date back more than 5,000 years. The Old Kingdom of Egypt, considered the birthplace of modern medicine, is credited for the first mention of medical practices including energy/vibrational healing. Each culture has a different name for the energy field and life force, such as Qi/Chi (China) or Prana (India). One of the most familiar early references to energy healing is the Biblical laying on of hands.

My explanations of the bio and subtle energy fields are simplified for this book. I encourage the reader to take advantage of the excellent in-depth books and online abstracts that are available for the study of these fields, such as James L. Oschman's *Energy Medicine, The Scientific Basis*, and Richard Gerber's *Vibrational Medicine, The #1 Handbook of Subtle-Energy Therapies*. Other resources are listed in my book's bibliography.

The word chakra in Sanskrit means *wheel* or *disk*. Chakras are understood to be receptors for the influx of energy from the Universal Energy Field and conductors of the energy flow from various layers of the biofield to all parts of the body. Quantum physics states that everything is made up of energy that constantly changes and flows.

Each chakra relates to specific physical organs, each has

individual characteristics and each is rooted along the spine both in front and back. Chakras can become compromised or blocked by physical, emotional, mental, or spiritual imbalances. These can manifest as physical symptoms related to a specific chakra. There are minor chakras located throughout the body that power the major chakras such as those in the joints, palms of the hands, and soles of the feet. Every chakra is a distinct color which radiates to corresponding auras encircling the body 360 degrees and reaching to approximately arm's length. The ancients saw chakras as vortexes of color and light, spinning at various speeds, and scientific research has shown this explanation to be accurate.

Because modern science now has the means to assess and evaluate vibrational healing hypotheses, energy therapy techniques are increasingly being accepted by the public for personal use and are being integrated into the medical profession as complementary care. Energy-based modalities include Healing Touch, Reiki, Traditional Chinese Medicine therapies (acupuncture, acupressure, Tai Chi, herbs), aromatherapy, reflexology, kinesiology, homeopathy, yoga, massage, sound "baths," martial arts, Emotional Freedom Technique (EFT), Energy Psychology, and related disciplines. Use of the subtle energy field consisting of chakras, auras, and meridians is frequently utilized in these restorative modalities.

Energy-based therapies are holistic in nature, treating the whole person physically, emotionally, mentally, and spiritually (PEMS). They encourage the body's natural healing systems to function more efficiently by promoting deep relaxation, stress, anxiety and pain relief, immune system support, relief of disease and medical treatment symptoms, while often deepening spiritual connection. The basic premise is that if a person is in balance, centered, grounded, and cleared, the probabilities for healing and recovery are significantly improved.

The seven layers of the Aura are:
- **P** – Etheric: Physical and closest to the body
- **E** – Emotional Body
- **M** – Mental Body connected with logic, reasoning, and thoughts
- **S** – Astral: Spiritual health
- **Etheric Template**: Psychic abilities
- **Celestial**: Intuition
- **Ketheric/Causal**: Life path

Each of the seven chapters of the book begin with listing the basic characteristics of a major chakra, its location, associated organs, capabilities if balanced, and physical symptoms if it is out of alignment. The meditations and stories are placed with related chakras and are offered as energetic "tools" to use for self-care and healing and to increase personal awareness.

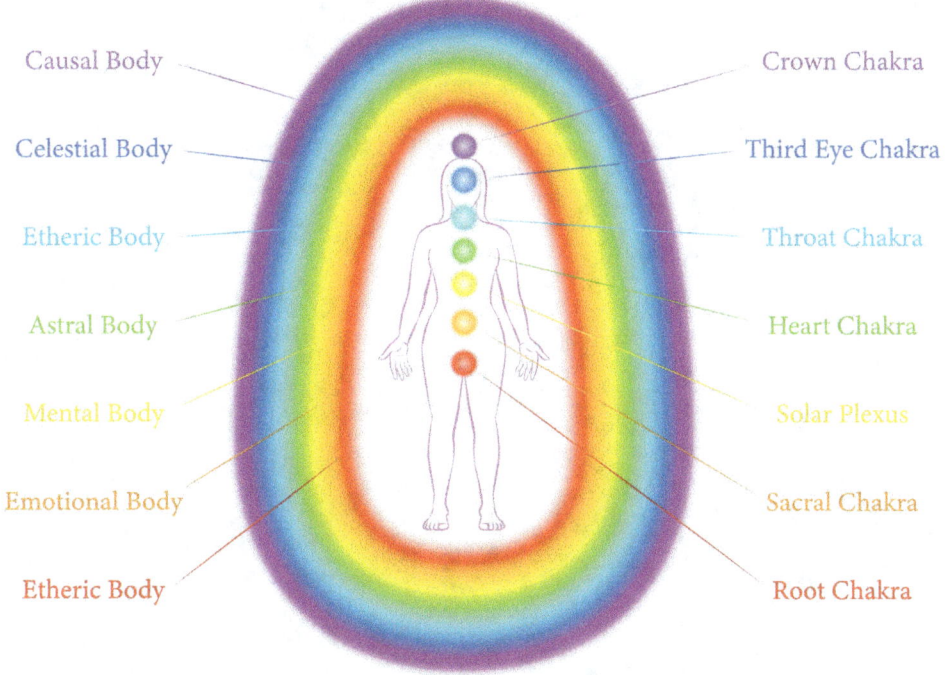

First Chakra (Root Support)

Family
Clan
Tribe
Group

Location: Base of the spine at the tailbone area.

Color: Red

Element: Earth

Anatomy: Prostate, Large Intestine, Spine, Back, Legs, Feet, Bones

Open (Balanced): Grounding, Energy, Life Force, Survival, Safety, Comfort, Basic Needs, Boundaries, Moving Forward, Stability, Power

Blocked (Compromised): Weight Loss or Gain, Urinary (men), Prostate, Fatigue, Poor Immune Response, Balance Difficulties

Affirmations:

I have close ties to my family, clan, and friends.
I am strong.
I take care of myself and am confident in all that I do.
I am balanced, centered, grounded, and safe.
My energy and life force are strong.

Earthing/Grounding Meditation

James Oschman, PHD, cellular biologist and physiologist, author of *Energy Medicine, The Scientific Basis,* states that multi-disciplinary research has revealed electrically conductive contact of the human body with the surface of the Earth (earthing/grounding) produces intriguing effects on physiology and health relating to inflammation, immune responses, wound healing, and prevention and treatment of chronic inflammatory and autoimmune diseases. It is believed that health benefits from grounding an organism include measurable differences in the concentrations of white blood cells, neutrophiles, lymphocytes, cytokines (which strengthen the immune system), as well as other molecules and chemical factors involved in the inflammatory response. Direct connection to the Earth and exposure to the Earth's electrons increases the electrical potential between body and Earth. With modern lifestyles, people have a disproportionate number of positive molecules due to their lack of connection with the ground partly, by wearing shoes and walking on pavements.

The use of mental grounding tools of meditation, visualization, stating affirmations, breathing techniques, prayer, journaling, music, reading, and expressing gratitude also benefit overall health by significantly reducing stress.

The earth/grounding meditation can be done outside or inside. If you can ground yourself outside by walking barefoot, lying, or sitting on the ground, do so as often as possible. When you cannot, sit in a comfortable position with your feet on the floor unencumbered by shoes.

Intention: To become centered, grounded, balanced, and cleared of energetic congestion.

Take relaxation breaths as you visualize yourself sitting on a chair outside in the warm sunshine or in the shade of a tree. Feel a breeze blowing over you. Allow your mind and heart to be completely at rest and at peace. Breathe deeply and slowly.

Picture roots coming out of the soles/souls of your feet and growing into the warm grass-covered Earth. What do they look like? How long are they? You are firmly connected to the Earth's magnetic field. Open yourself to allow Earth's healing energies to come into your body through the root system and completely fill all your cells.

Rest in the quiet of your heart, mind, and soul.

Repeat the visualization by picturing yourself lying on the grassy ground, absorbing the Earth's healing benefits.

Give thanks as you take relaxation breaths and focus on all that is good in your life. When you are ready, slowly bring your attention back to the present.

> *You must hold your quiet center,*
> *where you do what only you can do.*
> —Ha Jin "A Center"

The Mother Tree Meditation

In her book *Finding the Mother Tree*, Suzanne Simard identifies hub trees, or "mother trees," as the largest and often oldest and most connected trees in forests. Mother trees act as central hubs for vast below-ground mycorrhizal networks that communicate with young seedlings around them and accelerate their growth by making water and nutrients available to them through their respective root systems. It is known that trees form alliances and live in cooperative and interdependent relationships maintained by communication and collective intelligence.

Intention: To discover your mother tree and receive strength and gifts from her; to connect with humanity.

Take relaxation breaths as you visualize yourself on the edge of a dense, ancient forest. Breathe slowly and deeply as you are drawn to enter the woods, walking on a soft pine-needled path that is in front of you. As you begin to walk the path, you hear birds singing and see them flittering about. Squirrels are gathering nuts and scampering about. Light is filtering to the forest floor and beautiful wildflowers and ferns are growing nearby. The air is fresh and clear. As you walk deeper and deeper into the woods, you hear the rustling of leaves far above you, welcoming your presence and passing the word to your mother tree that you are coming. As you continue to walk deeper into the woods, you feel more and more peaceful, sheltered, and safe. You see your mother tree before you and become aware of her beauty.

Is your mother tree a sweet-smelling pine, the elder of the forest, the Wisdom Keeper?

Is it a maple representing the phases of life, an ally to help you move into a new chapter?

Is it a cypress or cedarwood, both representing love and humility, emblems of the heart to help you honor who you are?

Is your mother tree a redwood, sequoia, or another favorite "elder" tree?

Is your mother tree in a different classification or in a younger stage of life?

When you have time, research the properties of your mother tree, the gifts she is bringing to you.

As you approach her, place your hands over your heart and bow to her.

She has given you permission to sit at her base and to lean against her trunk. You feel fully supported as you do this. Are you sitting on moss? Soft needles? What does her trunk feel like? Does she have leaves or fragrant needles, flowers, or blossoms? If her roots are exposed, you may feel them comforting you.

Take relaxation breaths again. With every inhalation, you are breathing in her scent and nourishment. On exhalation, you are releasing stress, worry, and tension which she and the earth are absorbing. She is grounding you. Is there anything you want to tell her? Are there any questions you want to ask? Do that now.

Continue to breathe normally as you feel your mother

tree's strength, courage, resiliency, and stillness transferring into you. She is the nurturer of all around her. Her roots connect with other trees to give them sustenance, send messages, and help protect them. She both gives and receives.

While continuing to sit against her trunk, feel the root connection between your mother tree and the mother trees of all humanity. We live together in the same ancient forest. If one of us needs strength, courage, help or peace, it is guided to us by this strong root connection if we but ask. Consider how you could be a mother tree to friends and family. You can send this energy to anyone in the world who needs it.

Give thanks to your mother tree and for all the types of trees on earth. Give thanks for everyone who is reforesting and preserving our trees and environment. Ask for direction on how you may personally aid in this important and critical task.

Take several relaxation breaths, come back to the edge of the ancient forest and back into the present moment.

For the trees reflect who and how I can be
Standing tall, true, honest, and undeniably me
Unafraid to give, to love, to share, and to bend.
— Clare Dubois, author of *Where Trees Breathe* and founder of TreeSisters (treesisters.org)

Ancestors Meditation

In the broadest sense, our ancestors are the collective love, wisdom, and suffering of all the people who lived on Earth before us over the past 300,000 years or more. They are not limited to blood and family lineages. Connecting with our ancestors helps us understand who we are and our place in the larger ancestral community.

Intention: To honor your ancestors.

Take deep relaxation breaths. As you exhale send gratitude to your ancestors.

Breathe gently and think about who you are and where you are in this moment and season of your life. Visualize your family line, starting with a parent, sibling, or grandparent, allowing the person to come to mind. If you are adopted, remember someone who helped raise you.

Visualize an ancestor standing or sitting in front of you, sending the light of their wisdom into you. Ask if this ancestor has anything to share with you. You may simply feel a sense of quiet, calm, and peace. Offer your gratitude to your ancestor for having been a part of your life.

Choose another ancestor to visualize or be open to the

memory of someone who was important in your life such as a spouse, friend, or another person who has gone before. Remain open to their wisdom coming to you. Ask if the ancestor has anything to share with you. Offer your gratitude to them for having been a part of your life.

You may repeat these ancestral visualizations as often as you like.

"Messages" may come to you later in the form of images, thoughts, sounds, smells, feelings, remembrances, dreams, signs in nature, or in other ways.

Sit quietly to allow any other images to come to you. Following the meditation, you may want to journal any pictures, thoughts, or emotions you may be experiencing.

Know that you can call on your ancestors at any time for help. They are waiting for you to ask.

End the meditation with this simple phrase: "I thank all those who have helped shape and create me. I honor your divine wisdom."

End the meditation by taking relaxation breaths.

Our ancestors are an ever-widening circle of hope.
—Toni Morrison

Remembrance Meditation

None of us can go through life unscathed. All of us experience losses on our journeys. People who are important to us die, such as parents, a spouse, partner, siblings, and friends. Sometimes children or pregnancies are lost. Loss of a pet is painful. Physical abilities decline with age and we change cosmetically along with experiencing a decrease in stamina. Perhaps we have physical losses from an illness or through an accident. We may feel loss when moving from a home and neighborhood we loved. Some formerly meaningful relationships end in divorce, estrangement, or just fade away. The possibilities are endless. Coping can seem difficult.

Intention: To remember and honor a special person who was important in your life but is no longer present.

Sit comfortably. With relaxation breaths, breathe yourself into a state of feeling centered, balanced, and grounded.
What was your relationship to this person?
How did you feel physically, emotionally, mentally, and spiritually when you were in the person's presence?
How do you feel physically, emotionally, mentally, and spiritually with the person absent?

~ Judith Stoddard ~

In what way did the person's life impact yours? How were you changed by knowing them?

What did you love about the person? If the individual did something that hurt you, acknowledge it and let it go. There is no healing without forgiveness.

Express gratitude for your connection with this person and for having been in your life, for the growth and experiences you had by knowing them, for the skills learned and the blessings that are yours because of the person. Is there an act of kindness you can do to honor this person?

Sit in the quiet of remembrance as you take relaxation breaths.

Looking behind I am filled with gratitude.
Looking forward I am filled with vision.
Looking upwards I am filled with strength.
Looking within I discover peace.
— Quero Apache Prayer

The Healing Energy of Children

One afternoon, having just returned from the hospital during the crisis week following my elderly mother-in-law's knee replacement surgery, while she was in the ICU on life support after having strokes that followed the operation, I called our daughter and asked if I could have my grandson to play with for an hour. He was fifteen months old at the time and I brought him to our house and sat on the floor with him playing with a wooden marble run that had been made for me by a favorite uncle when I was a child. His joy at being with Grammy all by himself and playing with something special was soothing and calming for me, and his sitting on my lap as we ran marbles was more comforting than anything else I could have done. When a phone call came at the end of our hour of playing together, telling me that another crisis was happening, I was ready to return to the hospital to face it.

Before I had grandchildren, I joined a volunteer organization whose members read to preschool children. I volunteered because I was missing the joy that being with children brings to me. I didn't realize that what I was seeking was children's life energy that comforts and heals. It is a positive force—uncomplicated, pure, and shared unconsciously without strings attached.

The children I read to came from homes in a poor section of the city where few adults had the time or inclination to do one-on-one reading. I came away from these weekly sessions restored and happy, not just from their responses to the stories I had read with them but from the children making me laugh with the questions they enthusiastically asked: "Why do you have those things [wrinkles] on your face?" "How did you get so many of those [freckles]?" "What's wrong with your skin?" [It was a color different from theirs.] "How many little kids do you have at home?" [None at the time.] "Why not?"

~ *Judith Stoddard* ~

If you do not currently have children in your life, I encourage you to find some to connect with. You don't have to be especially fond of children or even feel completely comfortable around them. They will most likely feel comfortable with you. It helps if you can be silly and laugh easily.

We are fortunate to have three additional grandchildren in our lives, two girls and a boy, and all are loving spirits just like our first grandson. They are full of bounding physical and spiritual energy. They are sometimes challenging, as all children are, but they all give us precious gifts of time and fun. They are wonderful teachers.

To receive the healing energy of children, all any of us needs to do is be open and welcoming to the healing we are being offered, whether we understand it or not.

> ***There are no seven wonders of the world in the eyes of children. There are seven million.***
> — Walt Streightiff

Home Meditation

A home is defined as a house, apartment, or simply a place where someone lives. When home is a person, it is someone with whom you feel safe and secure no matter where you are. Home could be a person whose love you carry with you even if they are far away or may no longer be in your life. This meditation can be used for homes in which you no longer live but remember with love.

Intention: To consider the physical qualities of your home and your personal qualities that make others feel at home with you. To review Root Chakra qualities.

Ground yourself by taking relaxation breaths and sending energy to your Root Chakra. Picture your current home. What is the feeling you get standing outside your door? Is it welcoming? Could you make it more so?
What do you feel as you step inside? Is there a prevailing energy?
Do you have a favorite room? If so, visualize going there now. If not, choose another room or become aware of the room in which you are sitting. Are there objects that have meaning to you, gifts you have been given or mementos from

trips or vacations? Remember happy memories connected to them. Are there objects that no longer serve you that could be cleared?

What colors do you see? Often color choices reflect our personalities.

Does the room have a scent? If so, identify it.

Have you made a sacred space in this room? If not, is there a room or a portion of a room where you could do this by adding things meaningful to you and by setting the Intention for the space to become sacred?

What personal qualities do you exhibit that make people feel at home? Are you an attentive listener? Do you smile readily? How are you a welcoming presence? How do you set boundaries and protect yourself if you are with someone who makes you feel uncomfortable or unwelcome?

Bring your life force, groundedness, and energy to your Root Chakra, strengthening and expanding your Light and inner shining core. Infuse your home with this Light and your personal welcoming qualities and visualize sharing them with all who are homeless, migrants, refugees, children who are hungry or abused, or anyone in need of your help.

As you carry these personal qualities and your Light with you, consciously share them with all whom you meet on your path.

To close the meditation, take relaxation breaths as you give thanks for your welcoming gifts.

A Jewish Home Blessing

Through this Gate shall come no sadness;
To this dwelling shall come no trouble;
Through this door shall come no fear;
In this place shall be no conflict;
This home shall be blessed with
Harmony and Peace

— Anonymous

Leaving Home

Liminal — An adjective meaning: relating to a threshold or border between two things, states, or conditions.

Liminal experience — A transitional period between two phases of life, where you are neither in the previous phase nor in the next one. This concept is derived from the Latin word "limen," which means "threshold."

    I have never wanted to build a house, and I never wanted to live in an over-fifty-five community without children in the neighborhood. Never say never.

    We lived in a one-hundred-year-old Brandywine granite house for thirty-six years. Our children were four and seven when we moved in. It was a large home with deep windowsills, full of light, with beautiful woodwork and, for being located within city limits, a large yard. There were huge old trees on the property which gave shade in the summer with leaves that turned bright colors in the fall.

    The house was accommodating. During the civil war in Lebanon, we had friends come to stay as they left Beirut for safety. When our church burned down, the congregation held meetings in our home to make decisions about the future. The home was made for people, and having sixty there at once was an easy thing to do. It was a frequent gathering place.

    Because the house was more than one hundred years old, constant repairs were required. The chimney was rebuilt, all the rooms were painted several times, the roof and much of the wiring were replaced, the kitchen, two bathrooms, and powder room were remodeled, the cellar and garage floors and walls were recoated and a French drain was added. The old trees were slowly dying and had to be removed; young trees were planted to take their place. New second floor and attic windows were installed and wooden porch floorboards were replaced many times. We added wrought iron rails for the large double front steps, side deck, and back porch. A new furnace was installed, the air conditioner and hot water heater were both replaced twice, and there was other significant general upkeep. It was worth the expense, time, and effort. The home was beautiful, happy, and welcoming.

Our two children graduated high school and college from this home, and were married while living nearby, making our house home base. Both had two children while living on our block and often used our yard with kiddie pool, sand box, water table, miniature kitchen, and various toys as a playground.

The house saw frequent celebrations. There were years of Christmas Eve and Christmas Day dinners and breakfasts and the openings of presents. Two generations of children dyed Easter eggs, searched for baskets, single pennies, and plastic eggs containing coins. We sponsored a musicale for friends with professional symphony musicians and hosted countless neighborhood parties.

Then it all changed. Our adult children and their families moved off our block and out of the city. We always knew the years of living close together were a period of grace that wouldn't last, but we weren't prepared for the gaping hole their absences left in our life. Suddenly our home became too big. No one was stopping by on the way home from the park to swing on the porch swing, play with the toys, or have a treat. The house upkeep was harder. Now there seemed too many leaves to rake. The corner property sidewalks somehow became longer to snow blow, and we started to feel that the house was gently pushing us onward.

For two years I streamlined kitchen cabinets, cleaned out

closets, the cellar storage area and under the attic eaves, giving away items that were no longer needed to church bazaars. For two years we looked at city condominiums, apartments, and smaller older homes. Discouragingly, nothing felt right.

We noticed a new over-fifty-five development of townhouses being built just outside the city limits. The homes seemed narrow and small, but we kept checking on the building progress all winter. When the builder held an open house the weekend prior to settlement on two of the townhouses, we delayed a vacation trip so we could view them.

The first home's kitchen felt too small and the bedroom was on the second floor. The second house had a light, bright, large kitchen, and a sizable combination living-dining room. A master bedroom and bathroom as well as laundry area were located on the first floor. We loved it, chose a large end lot and made a deposit to hold it. The reality of making such a momentous decision was daunting.

This decision started an avalanche of activity. We went on vacation as planned, returned home and put our house on the market. Nineteen couples toured the home, and it sold within a month, necessitating our storing belongings and moving in with our daughter, husband, and children while our home was being built. During this crunch period, we were also making critical decisions about the building of our townhouse.

For a week after settlement I cried every time I was alone. I was crying because it was the end of an era, and we were leaving our beautiful, beloved home of so many years. I later discovered that each of our adult children had walked through the empty house by themselves to say goodbye, as we had done, before giving up their keys.

The new owners loved our home and cared for it well. They made changes I never would have made . . . the dining room was changed into a family room and the large living room was divided into a living-dining area. The trees we planted to replace the maple trees that had died were taken out and grass planted where ivy had grown. Do I mind? Yes, I do. Our son gently suggested that I was taking the changes too personally and reminded me that it wasn't our house any more. In my mind it will always be our family home.

We have an abundance of pictures taken in that house, of our children and grandchildren growing up, of parents and family now long gone visiting, and simply living happily there. As the song goes, "You can't take that away from me."

Do I miss that home? Sometimes. Do I wish we still lived there? No. We have moved on. We have built more than a house. We have built a new life with new and interesting friends while keeping our old ones. Celebrations continue. And it is home in the best sense of the word. It is very different, of course, but home nevertheless.

While our new home, too, is a liminal experience and space, I hope we won't be leaving home again anytime soon.

Body Scan Meditation

A body scan is a mind-body technique that helps a person become aware of physical and mental stress, tension, pain, or tightness. It helps us stay in the moment and can be done anywhere at any time. This meditation is designed as a seated scan that begins at the head but can be done while lying down and can be started anywhere in the body. If emotions arise, acknowledge them and let them float away. If they need to be addressed, do so after the scan.

Intention: To notice areas of the body holding stress or pain and to consciously relax them.

Sit comfortably. Gently close your eyes. Straighten your spine and feel the weight of your body on the chair. Place your feet without shoes on the floor. Rest your hands comfortably in your lap or on your thighs, palms up.

Begin by taking relaxation breaths, inhaling through the nose and exhaling through the mouth, making exhalation twice as long as inhalation. Exhaling through pursed lips will lengthen the breath. Feel a sense of relaxing more deeply with each breath.

Concentrate on breathing healing energy into areas of

stress as you do in meditation. Affirm that you are releasing unwanted anxiety and physical tightness as you become aware of each body area.

Begin at your head and face. Does your scalp tingle? Are you frowning, tightening your jaw, or clenching your teeth? Release these muscles as you breathe in and sigh away any tightness.

Tension is frequently held in the neck and shoulders. Lengthen your neck and drop your shoulders. Tilt your chin slightly downward as you breathe in energy and exhale to relax these areas.

Notice any sensations in your arms, hands, and fingers that need to be released. Breathe in pure energy and relax your limbs as you exhale.

Become aware of your chest area. Do you have any difficulty breathing? Do you feel tightness? Are respirations rapid or slow? Pay attention to your heartbeat. Holding the palm of a hand over the heart-lung area as you breathe deeply may help decrease respirations if they are too rapid. Patting the area in the upper chest firmly will also slow breathing.

Bring your attention to your stomach area. Is your stomach tight or tense? Do you feel butterflies or knots, signs of stress? Breathing into the lower abdomen, letting it rise on inhalation and softening with exhalation will help relax this area.

Notice your legs against the chair. Become aware of any pressure, pulsing, heaviness, uncomfortable tightness, strength, or weakness. Leaving your heels on the floor, make your feet go up and down to tighten and relax the calf muscles, which will release stress. Notice the sensations in the soles of your feet, the pressure, vibration, heat, or cold. Tighten and relax your toes. Massaging the feet also releases tension and pain.

Be aware of your whole body. Notice any remaining tension. Breathe into that area if needed and let it go. Tensing and relaxing muscles will relieve tension in that area.

Feel Earth energy coming into the soles of your feet and slowly move it upward through the body, connecting the Crown Chakra to the Universal Energy Field.

Take relaxation breaths and when you are ready, open your eyes and give thanks.

A body relaxation exercise beneficial to do at bedtime when ready for sleep:

Lie on a bed or the floor; take letting-go breaths at the beginning and end of this exercise.

The exercise may be done from feet to head or the reverse.

Breathe normally.

Tense your toes; hold thirty seconds; release.

Tense one leg; hold thirty seconds; release; repeat with other leg.

Tense trunk of body as best you can; hold thirty seconds; release.

Tense one arm; hold thirty seconds; release; repeat with the other arm.

Tense your neck; hold thirty seconds; release.

Shrug your shoulders; hold thirty seconds; release.

Tighten your face; hold thirty seconds; release.

Rest comfortably for a few minutes.

~ Judith Stoddard ~

From head to toe I was created for good things
Excellence and performance
All the best fit for kings
— Jason Tomlinson

Simplify Meditation

The Universal Law of Correspondence expresses the belief that there is correspondence between different levels of existence: whatever happens inside your mind is reflected on the outside. According to historians and language experts, the origin of the phrase, **"as above, so below, as within, so without"** first appears in a number of early medieval Arabic texts. The phrase suggests that the patterns and laws governing the Universe also operate within the individual. If this law is applied to "clutter," it infers that if our minds are cluttered, our surroundings and lives may also be cluttered. Studies show that clutter can cause depression, anxiety, and stress which in turn promote feelings of being overwhelmed. The reverse is true. Decluttering helps the brain process, organize, and increase memory storage, creates a sense of confidence, improves focus, creativity, and productivity, and improves health and well-being. Decluttering nurtures a feeling of freedom.

Intention: To become aware of what may be cluttering your life and consider ways of clearing them to make room for things you want to do, people you want to see, and opening mind space for new thoughts, ideas, and feelings.

Take relaxation breaths exhaling into a state of openness.

Decluttering Surroundings – Are my counters and work spaces stacked with papers and books? Do I empty trashcans regularly? Am I holding onto possessions that are no longer meaningful? Am I tired of dusting so many belongings and pictures or watering so many plants? How full is my attic, basement, or storage space?

Decluttering Closets and Drawers – Am I keeping clothes that no longer fit or are out of style? Do I have more linens or kitchen utensils, pans, and dishes than I need? What items that are stored in drawers can be reduced or removed?

Decluttering Devices – Have I kept email messages or texts longer than needed? Are my SPAM and deleted files overflowing? Are there icons of never-used phone apps I can remove from my screen? Do I constantly multi-task?

Mind Decluttering – Do I hold thoughts that upset or anger me, thoughts that do not help me? Would letting go of these thoughts allow me to live more in the moment? What might I do daily to help me declutter my mind, such as meditating, praying, reading a devotional, journaling, walking in nature, exercising, eating well, other pleasurable activities? Do I hold onto unhealthy relationships that could be mended or honorably ended?

Questions to help make decisions on what to keep:
    Does it hold happy memories?
    Could someone else make better use of it?
    Have I have worn or used it in the last year?
    Have I outgrown it physically or emotionally?
    Will anyone want to inherit it?

~ Finding Peace ~

Would I buy it again?
Can I decrease the number of similar or duplicate objects?
Do I need to own it? Could I borrow one if needed?
Is it good for the environment?
Most importantly, does it bring joy or have value for me?

Give thanks for this opportunity to appraise ways of decluttering and simplifying your life to ease stress and increase comfort and joy.

Anticipate a feeling of freedom as you take relaxation breaths and come back into the present.

Letting go of physical clutter also declutters mind and soul.
— April Williams

Full Moon Meditation

The Moon has always fascinated humanity. In the ancient world its brilliant presence in the night sky was the symbol of hope and personal illumination. As with the Sun, the Moon was associated with birth, death, resurrection, and fertility. The Moon was believed to control water and dreams, while its dark side was felt to be connected to the occult.

Reflecting upon the Moon's characteristics is a powerful way to tap into lunar energy. Connecting with the Moon grounds us and gives a sense of synergy with the earth and the cosmos. When the Moon waxes, increasing to full light, it offers a forward-moving energy and momentum that can help us work toward a goal or bring the first phases of a project to fruition. A full moon is a time of culmination, celebration, fulfillment, and gratitude. It offers an opportunity to recall something you would like to change and can be a time of letting go.

Intention: To be grounded, cleared, energized, and filled with gratitude; to find ways of moving forward and letting go.

As you take relaxation breaths, send each exhalation deep into your Root Chakra. Breathe normally as you visualize the bright light of the full moon bathing you in sparkling white light. This light is filling the room.

What would you like to change in your life? Ask for help in finding a way to move forward.

Is there something you would like to create in your life or are you creating something now?

Ask for help in finding a way forward.

Do you have something to celebrate? How can you acknowledge successes and joys?

Are you holding onto regrets? If so, release them.

Is there someone in the present or past you want to forgive for hurting you? If so, do it now. There is no healing without forgiveness.

Is there something for which you want to forgive yourself? If so, do it now.

Are there relationships or habits that no longer serve you? If so, consider ways to release them.

Recall things for which you're grateful. You may want to list them on paper or in a journal. Allow yourself to fully experience your gratitude.

Continue to feel the Moon's light in and around your body and the room. The light cleanses and restores you. Rest in the moonglow. Give thanks for the illumination you have received today and for your blessings as you take relaxation breaths.

The moon stays bright when it doesn't avoid the night.
— Rumi

Second Chakra (Sacral)

Creativity, Pleasure, Self-Expression

Location: Just below the navel.

Color: Orange

Element: Water

Anatomy: Large Bowel, Sexual Organs, Prostate, Bladder, Hips, Lower Back, Pelvis

Open (Balanced): Joy, Pleasure, Passion for Life, Creativity, Synchronicity, Power, Monetary Abundance

Blocked (Compromised): Bladder, Pelvic or Lower Back Pain, Low Libido, Lack of Creative Inspiration, Female Urinary Tract Infection, Anxiety, Power Struggles, Resentment, Greed, Dominion Over Others

Affirmations:

I am joyful and love to laugh.
I am passionate and creative.
I recognize and enjoy synchronicities.
I love my abundant life.
Many things give me pleasure and are fun.

The Five Senses Meditation

Our senses help us understand and perceive the world by relaying stimuli to different parts of the brain for interpretation. They help us make decisions, often keep us safe and living in the moment, and frequently increase our enjoyment of life.

Intention: To appreciate your senses and recognize their contributions to your life.

Take relaxation breaths and open into a state of awareness.

Sight is the most dominant sense. It is estimated that 80-85% of our learning comes through sight. What sights are beautiful to you, enrich your soul and make you joyful? What sights are disagreeable and painful to see but may move you to help others or take action?

Taste receptor cells make up our taste buds that register sweet, salty, bitter, sour, savory flavors in the brain but can also discern metallic, water, and fatty tastes. Smell, texture, and temperature aid in taste. Remember something wonderful you have tasted. What is your favorite food? Think of a new dish from another culture that you enjoyed. Do you have a special holiday recipe that you make or eat yearly? What tastes do you dislike?

Smell is the sense that most triggers memories. Think of a scent that would take you back to childhood or to a happy occasion. Do you have a favorite scent? What is its origin? Think of a scent that is associated with each season or is particular to the region where you live. Learn how to use essential oils to promote calm and healing.

Sound is thought to be the last sense that leaves the body during the dying process. A considerable amount of our communication is by sound. A "sound bath" using various musical instruments such as drums, chimes, and Tibetan singing bowls is considered a healing modality. What sounds may invoke joy or sorrow? Are there sounds around you now? Can you hear sounds of your body such as your breathing? Do you sing, play an instrument, or have a favorite type of music?

Touch transmits information to our brains registering pain, heat, and cold as well as softness, silkiness, roughness, itchiness, smoothness, pressure, tickles, and vibrations through our skin. Appreciate each of these sensations and consider where you might feel them. Studies stress the importance of skin-to-skin time in the first hour of birth. This early touch regulates babies' temperature, heart rate, and breathing, and decreases crying. It also increases a mother's relaxation hormone. Mothers and babies establish bonds with touch. Appropriate touch is important for all humans and animals.

Take relaxation breaths as you give thanks for your senses and for the aids that are available today to help augment hearing and sight when needed. Add anything regarding your senses for which you are grateful.

The five senses are the ministers of the soul.
— Leonardo Da Vinci

Laughter Meditation

    Laughter connects us to others and draws them to us. Forty to sixty percent of our "happiness factor" is thought to be genetic. The rest is dependent upon the environment. Genetics can be modified (e.g., heredity factor for high cholesterol can be improved by diet, exercise, etc.). Some researchers believe that laughter promotes health by boosting immune response, lowering stress hormones, easing anxiety and pain, improving mood, promoting relaxation and sleep, increasing blood flow, dropping blood sugar levels, relaxing muscles, helping defuse conflict, and promoting personal and group bonding. We often feel lighter after laughing.

    While sitting or standing, stretch your body by reaching upward as far as you can while opening your fingers wide. Repeat by stretching your arms to the front, then to the side. Bend toward either side in turn as you do this. Roll your shoulders forward, then backward several times. Relax facial and neck muscles. Take deep breaths and sit comfortably as you return to a normal breath pattern.

Intention: To remember times of laughter.

~ *Judith Stoddard* ~

Who are the family members, friends, children, or babies in your life that make you laugh? Give thanks for them.

Is there someone in your life who makes you laugh the instant you are together? What does that person bring to your relationship to trigger this laughter? Give thanks for the person.

Is there a movie that is especially funny to you? Is there a particular scene in a movie that always makes you laugh? Do you have favorite books or specific authors that are humorous? Give thanks for them.

Have you ever laughed aloud when by yourself while reading or watching something funny? Have you done this when someone else is in the room? Remember those times.

Was there a surprise occurrence, either positive or negative, that made you laugh? Have you laughed at a serious event such as a funeral? What caused this laughter? How did it feel to laugh at either of these instances? Remember times like these.

How does it feel to laugh uncontrollably? Can you think of a time when you laughed so hard you couldn't catch your breath? When was the last time you did this?

Be alert to Spirit's sense of humor: Murphy's Law incidents, humorous animals such as giraffes, zebras, monkeys, insects, and fish whose creations are more inventive than we could ever imagine. What else comes to mind?

Cultivate your sense of humor by not taking yourself too seriously. Laugh at yourself or negative situations rather than grumbling about them. Connect with people who have a strong sense of humor and place things that make you smile in frequently used areas. Think outside the box whenever possible. Consciously do something every day that makes you or others laugh. Smile.

As you take relaxation breaths, give thanks for your times of laughter and your sense of humor.

Stories and Poker

The Poker Club met once a month for years, rotating among five couples' homes. We loved it when it was our parents' turn to host.

As a young child I remember lying in bed listening to the rumble of talking, then bursts of laughter. The adults were telling stories and jokes while they played cards. When my brothers and I were old enough to listen and play, we were invited to sit in on the games. I was never brave enough to play cards with them but sit and listen I did. Jokes were told, but stories were most frequent, things that had happened in their daily lives. None of the stories were racist, off-color, or at the expense of others. Personal foibles were favorites.

Stories were part of our family DNA. Our father's background was Irish; mother's, Scottish. My father's sister and mother, one of our grandmothers, lived a half block from us, and I'm told that when I visited, which was often, I would walk in the door saying, "Tell me about the Olden Days." They would tell stories of the family's immigration to America, the 1919 influenza epidemic when a beloved twenty-one-year-old son and brother died, what the town was like with the anthracite coal mines in full operation, bulls running down the dirt street in front of their church, and other interesting and often exciting and funny stories, many being told while sitting on the porch swing together. I prodded my mother to tell stories of her growing up, equally as fascinating and often funny, and she did while working in the kitchen or relaxing in her favorite chair for a rare late afternoon rest. Long after I had children of my own I wrote these legacy stories and shared them with our children and my brothers and families so they wouldn't be lost.

As students in nurses' training, we passed along story

after story of funny, sad, or frightening incidents that happened while on duty; stories that circulated swiftly through our classmates' network. Medical personnel are notorious for laughing after taking care of a dire situation or emergency when anxiety is at its peak. Sometimes this laughter is misunderstood by patients and families, but it is a way the body and mind can relieve stress during a crisis. Who among us has not been to a funeral or memorial service where a humorous story is told resulting in the temporary relief of sadness by laughing before tears resume?

History repeats itself in our family gatherings as the stories begin. No devices are allowed. The grandchildren now join in, sometimes sharing a school or friend incident or concern. Funny stories are told by all ages. The teens and young adults still love to hear our stories of growing up when TVs and dishwashers were newly invented, party phone lines were in homes, typewriters were standard for schoolwork and, most stunning of all, that their parents were raised in cloth diapers (as we were). Most, though not all, family members are "tellers." All are avid listeners and wonderful laughers.

Stories are teachers of the human condition. Look for, listen to, and tell them, especially your own.

Sparkle Meditation

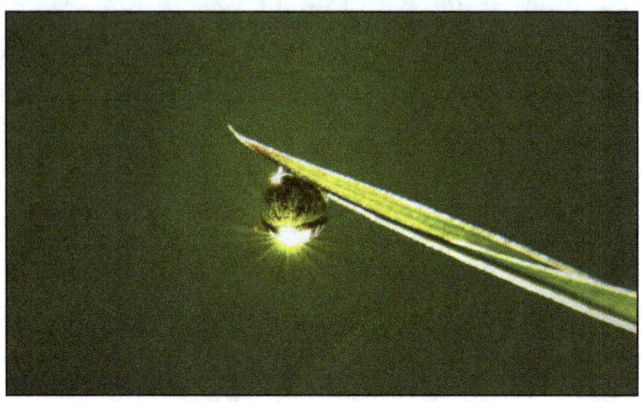

The word glitter comes from the Norse word glitra. Sparkle and glitter mean to send forth light, to bedazzle, glint, twinkle, shimmer, gleam.

Intention: To bring in Spirit's illuminating Light to clear and energize your energy field so you may sparkle and shine to help heal those with whom you come in contact.

Take relaxation breaths. On inspiration and exhalation, breathe the word center, then the word balance, then clear, then ground, then sparkle.

Visualize yourself sitting in a great Star of Light. Your Soul Light is being strengthened. This Light fills your body until you are completely lit from within and start to sparkle. The sparkles move to the energy field that encircles your body in all the beautiful chakra colors of red (Root), orange (Sacral), yellow (Solar Plexus), green (Heart), blue (Throat), purple (Brow) and indigo (Crown). The auras that emanate from your chakras are being cleared and becoming brighter and brighter. You are illuminated within and without.

Think of someone whose sparkle makes you laugh and feel joyful when you are with them. Remember a time or situation when that occurred. Give thanks for that person and experience.

To whom can you go when you feel your sparkle has temporarily dimmed? Could you help yourself regain some sparkle by meditating, listening to music, reading, journaling, exercising, eating something special, or watching a funny or favorite video?

Is there someone in your life who needs your sparkle right now? How can you share it with that person? Could you call, send a card, take the person to lunch, sit quietly with them, send Grace?

How can you become more aware of sparkle in others? What would you look for?

Sparkle needs to be cultivated and cared for. How can you do that?

Your internal and aura sparkles become tiny points of light that float into the air around you. Float them to people in your life who may be struggling. Mentally float them out into the world to places and people that need sparkles and light. Float them to any groups in which you are a member. Float them anywhere you desire. Rest in the peace of your sparkle and Light.

Sparkles gifts: dew drops, rain, ice, diamonds, crystals, fireworks, fireflies, fairy dust, tears, stars, magic, rhinestones, cosmetics, sequins, champagne, eyes. What else comes to mind?

End with relaxation breaths as you give thanks for your sparkle, however it exhibits. Be assured that even when you are gone, your Soul Light and remembrances of your sparkle will live on.

~ Finding Peace ~

Keep calm and sparkle on!
— Sarah Aronson

Maybe our sparkle comes from somewhere deeper inside, somewhere so pure and authentic and real, it doesn't need gloss or polish or glitter to shine.
— Mandy Hale

Sparkling Personalities

Archeologists tell us that humans used tiny mica flakes in cave painting to create a reflective glow. Ancient Egyptian, Chinese, Greek, and Roman civilizations also used them. The Egyptians created a glitter-like substance from crushed beetles. Although early versions of glitter were made with toxic materials, it has evolved over the years to become a less toxic decorative material. Nevertheless, these tiny particles are making their way into water sources and marine life is mistaking it for food, which in turn is damaging their health. Every tiny sparkly bit takes thousands of years to break down.

My humorous (I think) thoughts on how people may sparkle, depending upon personality types:

Extroverts are all snap, crackle, and pop. You can't miss their sparkle or their enthusiastic POP!

Introverts sparkle quietly inside. The sparkle is most definitely there, but you may have to look for it in their laughing eyes.

Ambiverts are the chameleons of sparkle. Having traits of both extroverts and introverts, their sparkle is always interesting, changing with their mood and situation.

Empaths (Highly Sensitive People) will be very aware of and understand the above personalities and their sparkle. They sparkle in their own lovely, sensitive ways.

These saying are often used as captions for photos. The authors are unknown.
(Source: https://kidadl.com/)

~ Finding Peace ~

"Spread the sparkle."
"Unleash your inner sparkle."
"Do more of what makes your heart sing, your eyes sparkle and your soul soar."
"Leave a trail of sparkle wherever you go."
"Don't let anyone dull your sparkle."
"Live with a little sparkle."
"Life won't sparkle unless you do."
"Glitter, sparkle, shine. But most of all be kind."
"Dream big, sparkle more, shine bright."
"Sparkle with all your heart."
"You were born to sparkle."

Rather than using physical sparkles or glitter, sparkle and shine in your own incomparable way.

Ken

My healing touch relationship and deepening friendship with Ken began with his first visit. He was in a stressful executive position in a nursing and retirement home and wanted to experience Healing Touch to help relieve stress.

Ken was very receptive to the modality and felt the energy move in diverse and interesting ways. The sessions were in the evening after his work day so the room's light was dimmed, lit only with candles and a salt lamp, creating a soft glow in the room.

The physical, energetic responses Ken experienced during the years we worked together varied. In almost all sessions he felt hands remaining on an area after I removed mine. Sometimes he felt hands on areas where I had not been working. He frequently felt a soothing warm blanket being put over him. Once, as I was doing a clearing technique, he felt pulling, then felt lighter as if he was being centered and balanced and his chakras were opening. In different session he felt the room was expanding and in yet another felt "sparkly energy" at his head and heart areas. In his mind's eye, he experienced seeing swirls of purple and green and points of light.

Ken had been very close to his grandmother and thought of her often during Healing Touch. "Presences" came to him often in his mind's eye. At times he felt them standing around the room, adults usually but children were included and once he felt them come in the door as the session started and circle the room. He didn't know any of these presences, but stated they were reassuring and comforting to him. I neither felt nor saw the presences.

In all sessions both of us could feel a strong amount of

energy moving, Ken throughout his body and I in my hands while doing the Healing Touch techniques. Sometimes the energy in the room felt soft and gentle and at other times heavy, dense, and powerful.

We had what I called The Laughing Session. In the middle of it, when Ken was in a deep relaxation state, he suddenly sat bolt upright, looked at me with wide eyes as though he had never seen me before, and I when I told him who I was and that he was okay, he crashed back down onto the table and back into deep relaxation again. I could hardly finish the session without laughing aloud, and when it ended and I had grounded him, he asked, "What was that?" and we both started laughing boisterously until we could hardly breathe. We laughed until he went out the door, and I continued laughing long after he was gone. It was a wonderful experience.

During the years of experiencing Healing Touch together every two weeks, I discussed with Ken how to set Intention, journaling, nutrition, qualities of essential oils, offered suggestions on how to be with the dying, taught him centering and balancing tools, and gave or loaned him books related to holistic self-care. We had deep discussions about his life and work. Ken frequently sent emails telling me that he was thinking more clearly, sleeping better, and felt a lot less stressed when in difficult situations and with decision making. He changed jobs during this time and felt confident during the interview and beginning the new job.

Ken felt that Healing Touch had come to him at just the right time and that our working together encouraged a period of growth. Ken felt nurtured by the Healing Touch sessions and felt I was a mentor to him. He believed that we have a whole universe supporting us, and he had new excitement regarding spirituality, God, hope, and the value of life itself.

Our last Healing Touch session before he moved to a

~ Judith Stoddard ~

new area and a different job felt "quiet" to him. Ken stated he could feel a circle of light being built around him and said the session felt like a blessing. I felt this way as well. Our sessions together were healing for us both.

A Spring Meadow Journey Meditation

A meadow is an open field covered by native grasses, flowers, herbs, and small plants that invite insects and small animals to make it their home. Spring is a hopeful time of rebirth and renewal.

Intention: To relax completely and bring joy and happiness to your Sacral Chakra center.

As you take relaxation breaths, consciously bring in new Qi (life force; pronounced Chee) from the energy field around you, making your exhalation twice as long as your inhalation.

Picture yourself standing on the edge of a beautiful meadow. You have chosen to come to this meadow alone. The meadow reaches as far as you can see. It has gently rolling hills that are covered with soft grasses and flowers. Blooming trees are in the distance.

It is a warm, soft spring day before the heat of summer arrives. You are dressed comfortably and carry a lovely blanket patterned in your favorite colors.

Take off your shoes and feel the warm grasses and earth on the soles of your feet as you walk into the meadow. You know exactly where you want to spread your blanket and you do that now.

Lie down on the blanket in a comfortable position. As you lie in the meadow enjoying the sun, you become increasingly relaxed and are aware of tension, anxiety, concern, and any pain leaving your body and mind. You feel at rest.

Notice the flowers that are growing nearby. You see small wild daisies and miniature sunflowers mixed in with purple and lavender violets. Sweet wild strawberries are within reach. Whatever flowers, plants, and grasses you see are there just for you. Enjoy and appreciate them. Continue resting peacefully.

A gentle breeze is blowing white and pink cherry tree blossoms onto you. You are being blessed. If there are bees or flying insects, they are going about their work and not bothering you. Are there birds or small animals nearby? You are completely relaxed and happy to be here.

Remember an experience from childhood when you were especially happy and joyous. Were you laughing? How old were you? What were you doing? Where were you? Were you with someone?

Breathe this memory and emotion into every cell of your body. The joy you are breathing in heals your spirit, body, and mind as you continue to rest on your blanket. You may stay as long as you like. Know that you can return to this sacred meadow any time you choose.

When you are ready to leave, stand, fold your blanket, and slowly walk to the edge of the meadow. Turn back to the meadow and give thanks for its restorative beauty, for the relaxation you have been given, for who you are, and for your life. Find things on this day that give you joy and offer that joy and happiness to others.

Take relaxation breaths and slowly return to the present.

~ Finding Peace ~

May the sun bring you new energy by day;
may the moon softly restore you by night;
may the rain wash away your worries;
may the breeze blow new strength into your being;
may you walk gently through the world and
know its beauty all the days of your life–
— Apache Blessing

Third Chakra (Solar Plexus)

Personal Power, Self-Esteem, Warrior Energy, Transformation

Location: Stomach Area

Color: Yellow

Element: Fire

Anatomy: Adrenals, Kidneys, Spleen, Liver, Metabolic and Digestive Systems

Open (Balanced): Gut level Intuition, Self-Confidence, Courage, Trust, Decisions to Move Forward, Determination, Strength

Blocked (Compromised): Eating Disorders, Food Sensitivities, Gastrointestinal Problems, Kidney Stones

Affirmations:

I have faith in my gut level instincts and follow them.
I am courageous.
I am trusting and strong.
I am self-confident.
I make decisions easily.

Luminescent Russanne

Russanne was luminescent in the way she lived her life, in her love for her family, in her faith, her courage and sense of humor, and she was physically luminescent as she died. Mary Catherwood wrote, "Two may live under the same roof for many years and yet never really meet and two others at first speech are old friends." From our first Healing Touch appointment Russanne and I felt we had known each other all our lives.

Russanne had been diagnosed with a rare uterine cancer. She had been referred to me by our son-in-law, who worked with her husband, Mike. Mike and their daughter came to our first Healing Touch session the day before Russanne was scheduled for surgery, thus beginning a three-year journey together that ended only with her death. In between our sessions, Mike became a wonderful ally as Russanne declined, keeping me updated with accounts of doctor visits, test results, how she tolerated treatments, and most importantly, how she was faring in general.

The initial visit was spent explaining Healing Touch, setting the intention to holistically prepare her for surgery, and doing a Healing Touch session. Russanne visibly relaxed and her color improved. Her chakras balanced, her energy field expanded significantly, and she stated that she felt much more ready to have the surgery. I taught her daughter a simple clearing technique to use immediately after surgery and in the recovery days following.

In the three succeeding years, Rusanne had radiation and chemotherapy and received medications supporting the treatments. Despite experiencing numerous side effects of these, she was able to take trips and to see both of her children married. One grandson was born during this time, and she joyously learned about a granddaughter's birth a few days before her death. She continued playing the organ at church, feeding the homeless, and helping others as much as she could.

At various times during our every-two-week sessions, she experienced a clearing of congestion, saw a bright light, felt a comforting finger on her forehead when I was not near her head, felt other hands on her head, felt warmth and tingling as well as other sensations. She always stated "It was good" and that she felt very relaxed. Once she said she had slightly opened her eyes, looked at me and "saw the face of an angel." She enjoyed the Healing Touch sessions and affirmed, "I get out of them whatever the Lord is intending for me, and so far they are uplifting."

Our times together often extended to standing or sitting on the porch chatting about our lives. Both of us wanted to prolong the visits. She was generous with gifts of flowers and a beautiful lighted angel that continues to grace my Healing Touch room.

Russanne's cancer receded several times with tumors shrinking, giving us hope of remission, only to progress with lesions being found in her lungs and eventually in her brain. The brain lesions caused a stroke, necessitating rehab to help her recover. Russanne said that shortly after the diagnosis she and Mike knew the end result. Nevertheless, she remained courageous, strong, and full of gratitude, humor, and love. Once or twice she shared that she felt depressed and anxious but quickly countered that she thought they were medication side effects. She was thankful for her life and felt very blessed.

I saw Russanne a day or two before she transitioned. She was in a hospital bed at home beside a window looking out into nature. She was receiving wonderful care and was in no pain. While she appeared to be unconscious, I spoke to her softly with my hands gently touching her, sending blessings and energy. Rarely have I felt more heart-centered compassion doing Healing Touch than throughout our time together, and especially during that visit.

Scientists are researching bioluminescence in humans, which is thought to be caused by chemical reactions and highly reactive free radicals produced via cellular respiration. There is empirical evidence that the human body literally glows. I had read about human bioluminescence during the dying process but had never seen it until the last day I visited Russanne. Her face shone as though there was a softly lit candle inside her head whose light was illuminating her beautiful face. A chemical reaction may have caused her glow, but I choose to believe she was illumined because she had lived her life in gratitude, light, and love.

A year into our Healing Touch journey together, Russanne turned to me and said, "I believe we were meant to be in each other's lives." I believe that too.

Courage Meditation

The origin of the word courage is from the Latin "cor" which means heart. Courage is commonly defined as being motivated by the heart to do something brave. Courage is taking a stand.

The Solar Plexus Chakra is a source of personal power and governs self-esteem, warrior energy, and the power of transformation. When in balance, a person exudes confidence, feels self-motivated, and has a sense of purpose.

Intention: To open, balance, clear, and strengthen your Solar Plexus Chakra.

Rub your palms together swiftly, creating static electricity. Place the palm of your right hand on your Solar Plexus Chakra, rotating your palm in a clockwise direction while repeating: "I am courageous, trusting, and strong." Repeat these steps two or three more times.

As you take relaxation breaths, visualize yourself sitting comfortably on warm, sparkling sand. Breathe in energy from the Sun and the surrounding energy field, strengthening your Qi, life force. Exhale this fresh energy into your Solar Plexus Chakra, supporting your natural gifts of warrior force, willpower, and courage. Breathe in what you feel you need. Your breath clears out congestion, fear, anxiety, worry, and anything that is blocking or dimming your personal power, creating a positive, energetic shift in your body.

Breathe normally as you visualize the lustrous yellow gemstone at the chakra's center spinning clockwise and bringing bright yellow light and energy into your auras. You are in an expanded, bright, and peaceful space. Sit quietly in that space.

Think of times when you witnessed or heard of acts of courage. Were they in your personal life as a child or an adult? Were they stories about family members or friends? Was there an uplifting incident in a recent news story when someone "stood up" or in a book you have read? Give thanks for these acts of courage.

Think of a time when you "stood up." Where were you? What did you do or say? Was it recently or in the past? Remember the details. How did you feel? Were there repercussions from your act of courage? If so, how did you manage them? Give thanks for your courage at that time. It strengthened you.

How can you be courageous during this time of strife in our country and the world? How can you stand up against injustice in any form? It takes courage for us to simply meet our own personal challenges in life—our griefs, fears, disappointments, hurts, physical pain, illnesses, or those of loved ones.

Send your clear bright Solar Plexus light filled with courage to places where there have been mass shootings, and strengthen those who are grieving and dealing with the grief of family or friends, and community losses. Send your courage to the police, emergency services staff, to nurses and doctors, and to anyone affected by those terrible acts of violence.

~ Finding Peace ~

Send your clear bright light filled with courage to sufferers of natural disasters, to war-torn countries, to refugees, migrants, the hungry and homeless everywhere.

Send your clear bright light of courage to anyone with mental or physical illness, to anyone in your own life who is struggling in any way.

As you take relaxation breaths, give thanks for your strength, courage, personal power, and sense of self. Find ways you can use your strengths in your daily life.

Courage is being scared to death but saddling up anyway.
— John Wayne

Courage is fear that has said its prayers.
— Anne Lamott

Energetic Sweeping Meditation

Physical and Mental Energetic Sweeping clears away old energy and makes a space for new. It helps release and remove toxins and congestion that may cause blockages in the energy system.

Intention: To clear the physical body and energetic field in preparation for new energy on all levels—physical, emotional, mental, and spiritual. To become filled with Light and to send it into your life and the world.

Take relaxation breaths, letting go of tension as you exhale.

Imagine a brush with exceptionally soft bristles—a paintbrush, hairbrush, or even a softly bristled scrub brush. Use whatever image comes to you. Brush from the top down* and from the center outward. This energetic sweeping meditation clears your powerful lymphatic system, which supports overall health, and your circulatory system. As you brush, thank each area or organ you are clearing for functioning effectively and keeping you healthy. If there are physical problems related to an organ or area, visualize clearing them with the sweeping and ask how you can help bring them back into health.

~ Finding Peace ~

Visualize brushing inside your head. Slowly and gently brush out any congestion that has gathered in your brain from concerns, worries, fear, anxieties, medication side effects—whatever is being stored there that is not helpful to you. Brush all areas of your brain, all the convolutions on the right and left sides, every process that regulates your body and mind. Brush behind your eyes, then your eyes, your nose, and sinuses.

Brush inside of your mouth and the tongue. Clear your throat by softly brushing from your mouth downward toward your stomach. Brush the inside of your stomach and the loops of your small and large intestines.

Brush inside the four chambers of your heart, then your bronchi and lungs, the right lobes, then the left. If you are a woman, brush your breasts in a circular motion, moving congestion outward.

Brush your liver (right side of body), pancreas, gallbladder, and spleen (left side). Brush your kidneys and the adrenal glands that sit like little caps atop them. Brush the inside of your bladder and urinary tract. Brush your pelvic organs, ovaries, and uterus, if female. If they have been removed, brush that space. Males, brush the organs specific to your gender.

As we clear, stagnant energy is brushed into the lower extremities. Brush down your right leg, moving all congestion into Mother Earth through the soles of your feet. Repeat on your left leg.

Using your hands, and starting at the energetic field around your head, gently brush your auras, continuing down the outside of your body from head to feet. Visualize clearing 360 degrees around your body. The auras become bright and clear as you do this.

At the Crown Chakra, bring in liquid Light from the Universe. It flows into all the organs and areas that were cleared.

~ Judith Stoddard ~

You are now filled with Light and are glowing. This Light strengthens all your chakras. Send the liquid Light in your Solar Plexus Chakra to anyone in your life who is struggling and to anywhere in the world where it is needed.

Rest in this glowing peace. Give thanks for the feeling of being open and clear. Take Relaxation breaths to end.

*This meditation may be done in reverse from the feet upward, releasing into the Universe.

When you let go you create space for something better.
> — Anonymous

Spider Spiritual Symbol Meditation

Spiders have been on earth for 300 million years, humans only about 2.8 million. They are in the mythology and folklore of cultures around the world. Archeologists believe webs probably inspired the making of nets for hunting and fishing. Native American Indians used webs on wounds to stop bleeding. Spiders' bodies are a symbol for infinity.

Spider symbolizes feminine energy and is considered the Divine Mother or Grandmother, creator of the world. She is the weaver of life's fate, of manifestation, holder of ancient wisdom, creativity, balance, interconnectedness, patience, receptivity, fortitude, and an anchor. In one myth, she is credited for creating the alphabet, and in another for capturing the Sun for the world. She also symbolizes the shadow side, the side of us we may want to hide. She encourages us to connect with the shadow side and not fear it, allowing us to be truer to ourselves.

Intention: To become aware of Spider's qualities and how they could be incorporated into your life.

Using your forefinger, draw the symbol for infinity (the number eight lying on its side) on your forehead as you take relaxation breaths.

~ Judith Stoddard ~

Creativity – How is creativity manifesting in your life? What could you do to become more creative?

Connections – Consider how you connect with others. Could your skills be enriched?

Patience – Reflect on a difficult situation that recently tried your patience. What tools did you use to cope? Could you have managed the situation differently? What did you learn from this opportunity?

Receptivity – How are you receptive to others? Are you a good listener, welcoming diverse ideas or suggestions with an open heart and mind?

Anchor – Are you an anchor for people? Who are anchors for you? Review how you stay grounded and balanced.

Fortitude – Has the shadow side, the dark side of Spider's traits been evident in your personality and in your life? Are you becoming too close to an entangling situation?

Imagine a beautiful shimmering web that holds Spider's attributes. Use it to connect to family, friends, and anyone who needs your gifts. The most important message from Spider is that you are an infinite being who will continue to weave patterns of life and living. Anything is possible.

As you take relaxation breaths, give thanks for the feminine energy and attributes that the Spider totem symbolizes and offers to you.

Spider . . . weaving webs of delight, weave me a peaceful world, carrying creation in your web waiting to be unfurled!
— Anonymous

Tuning in to Yourself Meditation

We often race through our day thinking only of our busy schedules, what we need to do next, where we are required to be, and how we will manage our responsibilities to accomplish what is necessary. This meditation is designed to encourage slowing down, enjoying the moment and becoming aware of how you are. The day goes more smoothly and we achieve more by taking even a few minutes to breathe consciously and tune in to ourselves, both at the beginning of day, as it progresses, in the evening and before sleep.

Intention: To tune in, assess, affirm, and care for yourself.

Center and ground by taking relaxation breaths.

Feelings – What feelings are you currently experiencing? Acknowledge and examine them.

You cannot make yourself feel something you do not feel, but you can make yourself do right in spite of your feelings.
— Pearl S. Buck

Needs – Do you have a need at this moment? If so, what can you do to meet the need?

~ *Judith Stoddard* ~

When you realize nothing is lacking,
the whole world belongs to you
— Lao Tzu

Just "Being" – How can you just "be"? Does the thought of not accomplishing anything major today make you feel uncomfortable? Can you give yourself permission for self-care, including "just being"?

In today's rush we all think too much, seek too much, want too much and forget about the joy of just Being.
— Eckhart Tolle

Regrets – If you are holding onto regrets, tie them to a colorful kite, fly it and let go of the string. They are not helpful to you. The Universe absorbs regrets and turns them into Light. Doing this makes room for personal growth.

Don't regret what's happened. If it's in the past, let it go.
Don't even remember it!
— Rumi

The soul always knows what to do to heal itself. The challenge is to silence the mind.
— Caroline Myss

Laughter – What makes you laugh? How do you play? What can you do today to feel joyful?

A day without laughter is a day wasted.
— Charlie Chaplin

Affirmations – Affirm your wonderful qualities. You're the best! Take it to heart and remind yourself of your positive attributes often.

~ *Finding Peace* ~

Owning our story and loving ourselves through that process is the bravest thing that we'll ever do.
—Brene' Brown

One of the best feelings in the world is knowing your presence and absence both mean something to someone.
— Unknown Author.

**Be happy in the moment, that's enough.
Each moment is all we need, not more.**
— Mother Teresa

Rest in this present moment and peaceful space.

Give thanks for all your blessings and gifts. Take relaxation breaths to end the meditation.

If you feel sad, give yourself permission to accept and walk through it. Feeling down will usually pass with self-care. If it lingers, consider getting professional help.

Consciously do something to care for yourself daily.

Suggestions for self-care:
- Use lavender and other pure essential oils for health and stress relief.
- Make a gratitude and blessings list.
- Meditate.
- Have a tune-up with an energy worker; get a massage or facial.
- Do anything fun that makes you laugh or feel joyous.
- Tell someone you love them.
- Have lunch or coffee with a friend or new acquaintance.
- Call friends if you can't meet with them. Send cards or notes.
- Complain when you need to but release the complaints into the Universe after stating them.

- Wear bright colors.
- Walk mindfully; do any other exercise you enjoy.
- Listen to favorite music. Sing and dance!
- Read a daily devotional, good book, watch a movie, read poetry
- Journal.
- Smudge your home with sage for clearing.
- Cut back on or omit sugar and alcohol (seriously? Yes). Chocolate is excluded.
- Give gifts. Receive them graciously.
- Use Affirmations to acknowledge your positive attributes.
- Eat out/bring in. Make a new and unusual recipe.
- Buy something special and frivolous such as special tea, fancy food, or an item of clothing.
- Take naps.
- Take educated risks; do something outrageous and out of character.
- Learn something new.
- Donate money and/or time to a worthy cause.
- Share your special gifts.
- Buy a tee shirt that reads "It's all about me."

It is difficult to help others if we are not balanced and in alignment ourselves.

> ***No matter how much chocolate you eat,***
> ***your earrings will still fit.***
> —Anonymous

Journey Into Wellness,
An Opportunity for Self-Healing and Learning

In mid-September 2011 I returned from a two-week trip to Scotland where I had been in full health and able to hike daily. The first weeks at home found me exhausted and not able to recover from what I thought was jet lag. I suddenly became very ill with viral symptoms of severe headache, body pain, and loss of appetite. After numerous blood tests, I was diagnosed with Epstein-Barr, the virus that causes mononucleosis. By mid-October all the viral symptoms had left except exhaustion, but I began to have extreme shortness of breath, severe coughing, and a high temperature in the late afternoon and evening, which broke in the middle of the night with profuse sweating. An X-ray showed that I had pneumonia in both lungs, and I was started on an antibiotic. The symptoms abated, but returned after I went off the medication. I was given a second round of a broad-spectrum antibiotic. Coughing and shortness of breath continued, and a second X-ray showed the pneumonia was progressing. Extensive blood work as well as chest, abdomen, and pelvic scans were ordered. During Christmas week I had an appointment with a pulmonologist, who immediately scheduled a bronchoscopy. The biopsy diagnosis was a rare, life-threatening, non-contagious inflammatory pneumonia. The viral assault on my body caused my immune system to turn against itself, allowing organizing inflammatory tissue to start filling my lungs. I was prescribed three months of massive doses of prednisone. This started my journey into wellness.

Prednisone can have unpleasant side effects. When I brought my prescription home, I placed it against a rose quartz crystal and salt lamp for clearing, and every morning when I took a pill I thanked it for its healing properties and asked that it cause as few side effects as possible. Because I was immuno-compromised and feeling unwell, I spent much of my time at home, so I had more occasion to concentrate on the healing self-care tools of meditating and daily journaling, including a healing a mantra, visualizing, and having sessions with an energy worker who was also a reflexologist and aromatherapist. I read supportive and fun books, listened to my favorite music, watched uplifting movies, and welcomed anything that made me laugh. Other than when I was contagious with the virus, I was able to continue my Healing Touch practice and felt peaceful and at my best physically during sessions. I knew the energy of sessions was healing me as well as the client.

This five-year illness provided opportunities for learning that I would not have had otherwise. It gave me a better understanding of and appreciation for the exhaustion caused by serious illnesses and treatments, and the frustration of a chronic or long-term illness. I experienced an insulin-produced uncontrollable hunger caused by large doses of prednisone. The rare pneumonia returned twice in the following years after my lungs were thought to be permanently cleared, necessitating repetition of prednisone treatment. The third time it returned, prednisone dosage and length of treatment were increased. Because there is a possibility of the pneumonia lying dormant, I remain on low dose maintenance medication. Though slightly scarred and compromised, my lungs remain high functioning and clear.

There were hard lessons learned during these years, but this challenging illness reaffirmed my belief that by combining restorative holistic and spiritual practices with excellent medical care and strong family and friends' support, the curative process can be accelerated.

And now? I'm dealing with another rare and (possibly) life-threatening blood-related autoimmune health challenge

~ Finding Peace ~

that developed after having a severe case of Lyme disease. My Intention is to remain strong and well and to continue to use all the holistic healing techniques in my toolbox that have so enriched my life. The axioms "Live one day at a time" and "Appreciate the present moment" sometimes feel trite, nevertheless they remain helpful reminders as the journey continues. And I try to keep laughing.

Self-Created Affirmations Meditation

Affirmation (one definition) – Positive personal thoughts and encouraging, confirming statements. When repeated and believed, affirmations can help make positive changes by overcoming self-doubt and negative feelings. Empirical studies show that self-affirmations may mitigate the effects of stress.

Intention: To become aware of personal strengths and gifts.

As you inhale during relaxation breaths, breathe in the pure energy around you and exhale it into the Solar Plexus Chakra. Repeat this breathing until you feel centered and grounded.

How do you feel when you affirm?:
I am adventurous. Is there a time when you did something adventurous? What did you do or where did you go?

I am a comfort to others. Consider ways in which you are a comfort.

~ *Finding Peace* ~

I am beautiful. Remember a time when you felt especially beautiful inside and out. Discard self-criticism.

I am enough. Repeat.

I am humorous. How are you funny? Evaluate your sense of humor. Look for ways to share it.

I am free. Reflect on ways you feel free.

I am ingenious. What ideas have you had that were so creative you could hardly believe it yourself?

I am strong. What specific strengths do you have?

I am valuable. To whom are you personally valuable? What are you doing in your life that is of value?

I am wise. What gifts of knowledge do you share with others? Can you find more ways to do so?

What other affirmative words resonate with you?
Express daily personal affirmations.
Give thanks for all your blessings and gifts as you take relaxation breaths

> *I sometimes forget I was created for joy.*
> *My mind is too busy*
> *My heart is too heavy*
> *for me to remember that I have been called*
> *to dance the Sacred dance of life.*
> — Hafiz, Persian lyrical poet

Superpowers Meditation

The word Superpower may evoke images of superheroes' powers of being able to leap a tall building in a single bound, see with X-ray vision, break up asteroids before they hit the earth (Superman), regenerate limbs, stick to ceilings and the sides of buildings (Spider-Man) have a Lasso of Truth and the ability to stop wars (Wonder Woman). We may not have any of these extraordinary powers, but we have or can cultivate capabilities that all superheroes have in common such as strength, resiliency, heroic action in circumstances of injustice, and adherence to strict moral and ethical codes.

Intention: To be conscious of your Superpowers and honor them.

Take relaxation breaths, breathing in energy from your field and exhaling it into the Solar Plexus Chakra, seat of personal power and self-esteem.

Journaling answers to the following questions may help define or remind you of your individual Superpower gifts. Sometimes simple things that you do easily are Superpowers, but you may not think of them as such. Superpowers are personal gifts that should be honored.

- Who are you? How do you see yourself?
- For what are you supremely qualified (your main Superpower)?
- What is something you really love to do? Do you use the skill/talent in your daily life? If not, could you? If you use it for others are they transformed as a result? If so, how?
- What achievements have made you the proudest so far in your life? What was the process that contributed to these successes? What strengths and abilities did you use? What parts did you like best?
- How can you use your Superpowers to continue to move forward? How will they contribute to the quality of your life and other's lives?

Discern what matters to you:
 I am at my best when I . . .
 I am at my worst when . . .
 I am genuinely happy when . . .
 I want to be a person who . . .
 The things that matter the most in my life are . . .
 The qualities that I admire most in others are . . .
 My greatest talents and best gifts are . . .
 The most admirable thing about me is . . .
 People who know me well think I am good at . . .
 What I really do best is . . .

 Place your writing where you can add more thoughts as they arise while you remember and reflect upon your Superpowers.

 Give thanks for your empowering gifts and ways you can use them in your life to empower others. End with relaxation breaths.

~ *Judith Stoddard* ~

We can't help what we are, only what life we choose to make for ourselves.
— Wonder Woman

This meditation is based on *Vision Exercises for Leaders* by Carolyn Maue, Executive Coach and Consultant, The Maue Center (carolyn@mauecenter.com). Carolyn authored *Gourmet Leadership, Turn up the heat on your secret sauce.* The content and revisions are used with permission.

Fourth Chakra (Heart)

Love, Compassion, Emotional Balance

Location: Center of Chest

Color: Green

Element: Air

Anatomy: Heart, Cardiac Plexus, Thymus Gland, Lungs, Breasts

Open (Balanced): Gives and Receives Love, Compassion, Empathy, Forgiveness, Healthy Grieving

Blocked (Compromised): High or Low Blood Pressure, Heart and Lung, Problems, Unexpressed Grief Issues

Affirmations:

I love people and am open to receiving love.
I am compassionate and empathetic.
I am open to trying to forgive.
I open my heart to my grief and to other's.
I freely express emotions when it is fitting to do so.

Butterfly Blessings Meditation

The word Blessing has many meanings. It could be used in giving thanks before a meal, a benediction at the end of a worship service, an endorsement or permission, or, as in this meditation, to acknowledge happy childhood experiences.

Intention: To center, ground, and remember summer childhood blessings and share them with children who are hurting.

Take relaxation breaths, letting go of stress, fear, and tension on exhalation, opening to memories and to ways of sharing them.
Visualize many-colored butterflies around you. Stay still so they may land on you.

Remember ice cream and popsicles. What were your favorite flavors? Where did you get these treats? Attach the memory to a colorful butterfly and send it to a meadow with beautiful wildflowers.

Remember swimming. If you had the opportunity to swim, where did you go? If it was in a pool, remember the smell of chlorine and the happy laughter and the splash of water. If it was in the sea, remember how salt water made your skin and eyes feel. Remember being gently lifted by waves. If you swam in a lake or river, remember the color of the water, the clouds and sky above, and perhaps the smell of mud on the bank. How did your toes feel on the bottom? Was it sandy or muddy, were plants touching your toes and legs? Attach the memories to butterflies and send them to your meadow.

Remember boating. Did you canoe, kayak, sail, travel on a ferry? Send those memories by butterfly to your meadow.

Remember vacations. Did you have a favorite place to vacation? Did you attend a camp or go camping? Did you travel to a new area? Visualize a past vacation and remember where and when it was. Who were you with? Attach the memory to a butterfly and send it to your meadow.

Remember learning something new. Did you learn how to swim, ride a bike, play a game, roller skate, or another new skill? Attach the memory to a butterfly and send it to your meadow.

Remember fresh fruit and vegetables. What produce did you eat in summer that wasn't available in winter?

Remember flowers. Did you grow flowers, buy them at a farmers' market, enjoy them in your neighborhood, or see them as you traveled in a car? Attach these memories to butterflies and send them to your meadow.

Did you read books? Have special friends? Catch fireflies? Go to Saturday movies or an amusement park? Have a job you liked? Remember all these and attach them to butterflies and send them to your meadow.

~ Judith Stoddard ~

Go to your meadow. Gently gather butterflies that are carrying your memories on their wings and send them into the world. Attach any concerns you have and let them flutter away. Give thanks for the gifts and memories, happy or sad, that you received growing up that made you the person you are now. End the meditation with relaxation breaths.

A Blessing is a circle of light drawn around a person to protect, heal and strengthen.
— John O'Donohue,
To Bless the Space Between Us

Gift of the Day

Quite a while ago I began a practice that I call "Gift of the Day." The only requisite is that it is something out of the ordinary and startles me into voicing or thinking, "Whoa! Wow!" or "Oh!"

Some recent Gifts of the Day were a red fox crossing the street in front of me and then turning around to lock eyes for a few seconds before running into the woods, a broken robin's egg shell balancing on a split rail fence, caught as it fell, a small bunch of wild pansies blooming in a wedge of dirt on the outside corner of a garage door, and a brilliant sunrise I enjoyed one morning when I arose earlier than usual.

A Gift of the Day may be a synchronistic experience, a job offering or prospect arriving unexpectedly, meeting or meeting again someone who changes your life, something in nature, or any delightful surprise. These gifts may seem minor when they happen, but in hindsight were of earthquake-like magnitude. They may also elicit a "Whoa! Wow! Oh!"

Research is being done on the health benefits of expressing gratitude. Our everyday gifts are too numerous to calculate and may not be noticed because they seem so common. Opportunities to become aware of some of these everyday gifts, as well as your personal gifts and suggestions on how to share them, are offered inside this book as you read it page by page or open it randomly. They are gifts I give to you.

But The Gift of the Day is yours alone. It is waiting for your notice, exclamations, and thanks.

Gifts from the Heart

It is hard to decide which Christmas was my favorite. Was it the one when Santa brought the beautiful bride doll? Or the ones where I received the dollhouse and marble run made by my uncle, both of which were enjoyed by our children and grandchildren and which still live in our home? Or was it the Christmas when I was eight and my grandmother sewed a sky-blue quilted bathrobe with pink cabbage roses that I found hanging on my doorknob when I awoke?

Certainly one of the happiest and most special was the December our daughter was born. Another was the fun Christmastime when our son sewed scrunchies for fastening his sibling's long hair and called it "The Sister Series." My husband and I spent freezing cold Christmas Eves in the basement late at night trying to make train tracks stay together, putting together a two-wheeler bike with directions in Polish and advice in English that said, "Assemble before using," and completing other challenging, last-minute projects for Santa to leave under the tree. These Christmases are also memorable because of the change in our family's concept of gift giving— from *buying* gifts to *making* them or doing something special for each other. Our gift giving became more personal.

One long ago November a local journalist published an article about Gifts from the Heart. She suggested giving creative coupons instead of gifts, such as promises to do chores and household tasks, for making special foods and meals, and gifts of time together. Our daughter was thirteen years old that year and our son nine and a half. Neither had much money to spend for gifts. We began giving coupons that year and have continued to give them at Christmases, and on birthdays and anniversaries since then.

Most coupons had elaborate drawings on them. They

~ *Finding Peace* ~

were designed on scraps of paper found around the house, special handmade cards on construction paper and frameable poems on eight-by-ten-inch stock paper (one of the most memorable was about my refusing to use a pressure cooker. This from our adult daughter).

A few examples of coupons given and received over the years are listed. They always begin with:

This Coupon Entitles you to . . .
- A roll of film being developed, I'll pay.
- Free cleaning of the living room, toy room, all bathrooms, kitchen, my room (a $20 value).
- A free "End of discussion!" (that one had an expiration date).
- A free candlelight dinner made by us. Afterwards a peaceful evening.
- A *peperment paddy** (peppermint patty) a day for 1 day, nah, make it a weak, * or seven of them at once.
- A free Vaseline lip therapy thing (ChapStick)
- A faithful dieting & aerobic companion after January 1.
- A root beer float . . . or whatever; I'll treat
- A free kiss or five free hugs
- A chicken dinner at Granny's Inn for a carbohydrate blitz on Parent's Weekend at college; you may foot the bill (picture of a foot included).
- One trip to a museum without complaining.
- One "I call green chair!" (the recliner in the TV room; brother to sister or sister to brother).

Giving Gifts from the Heart coupons has made all of us more thoughtful about gift giving. It has been fun for all of us, often elicits laughter and is a tradition that I hope will live long in our family. And perhaps in yours.

*Original spelling

Caring for the World's Children
Heartstrings and Energetic Cords Meditation

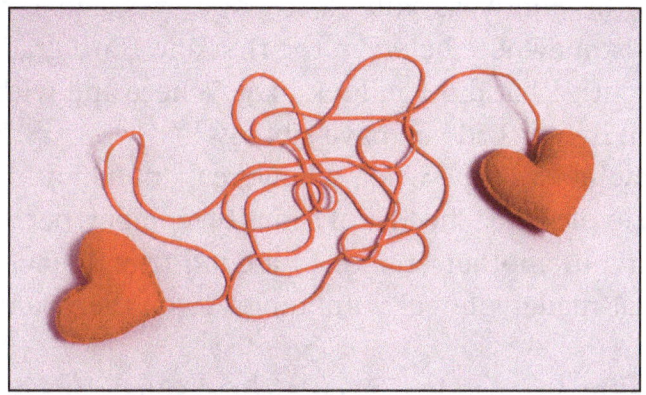

Heartstrings: used in reference to one's deepest feelings of love or compassion.

Physically, heartstrings refer to the chordae tendineae, a group of tough, string-like tendons in both ventricles of the heart that connect the papillary muscles to the tricuspid and bicuspid valves of the heart. They hold the heart valves in place while the heart muscle contracts and pumps blood from the chambers into the arteries. They are made of strong collagen protein fibers but also contain elastin protein fibers to provide elasticity and cells to repair the protein fibers.

Energetic Cords are invisible threads connecting people to other individuals. They are spiritual "ropes" that attach one person's life force or aura to another person's life force or aura. People are born with some of these cords and attach others throughout life. Negative cords attached to a person or situation, present or past, may be mentally cut with silver scissors, with the Intention of letting them float away, freeing the person from them.

Intention: To send comfort and love to children of the world by extending Energetic Cords from your heart center to theirs.

~ Finding Peace ~

Place your hand over your heart to feel it beating as you take relaxation breaths, and ask for it to be filled with Universal Love.

Breathe gently as you close your eyes and remember yourself somewhere between the first and third grades, ages six to eight. What did you look like? Where and with whom were you living? Did you have siblings?

Remember a time when you were ill, unhappy, or afraid. Did you experience the loss of a family member, pet, the grief of moving to another area or of a good friend leaving, anything that made you feel vulnerable? If so, then name those feelings.

Was there a person who comforted you during this time? Did you have a favorite doll, pet, toy, or blanket to hold onto? Place that feeling of being comforted into your heart center.

Stretch your heartstrings of comfort and love, attaching them to the heart centers of children:
- in your city, state, country, and all around the world who are unloved, lonely, helpless, or vulnerable in any way
- who live in unhappy or dangerous homes
- who are abused physically or mentally
- who are homeless or hungry
- who are struggling with disabilities or are being bullied
- who are in hospitals and are ill, injured, in pain, or undergoing chemotherapy or surgery
- who have lost parents, other close family members or pets

Is there a child in your life who is struggling? Attach your heartstrings to them and send comfort and love. Try to find ways of helping that child through the difficulty.

Perhaps you are hurting, fearful, sad, or are feeling vul-

~ *Judith Stoddard* ~

nerable. Is someone comforting you with their energetic heartstrings of love? If not, how and to whom can you reach out to ask for help?

Give thanks for the opportunity to share your compassion with the world's children.

End with relaxation breaths.

Children make your life important.
— Erma Bombeck

My Mother Was Buried in a Cookie Jar

The day before our daughter was married, my mother rapidly declined mentally. She was ninety years old and had been having memory difficulties for several years but was able to continue to live on her own in the large family home where we grew up. My older brother and wife lived in the same town and graciously oversaw her health, finances, and house upkeep.

One of her oldest and few remaining friends died suddenly and it threw Mother into a confused state. When my older brother called to say she would not be able to come down for the wedding, I cried, knowing that life had shifted permanently.

Over the next few years, Mother remained at home with day help. My younger brother and my family rotated weekends to cover her care while my older brother and wife continued to oversee organizing professional weekly care. They also stopped by daily to check on her. She remained in good physical health, but her mind slowly continued to deteriorate. Mother eventually went to live with my younger brother and his wife. She lived with them for two years until she had physical problems and could no longer be cared for at home. She was moved to a nursing home with assisted living care where her life ended two years later.

Mother had been a nurse and had always prided herself on not eating sweets and on eating a good breakfast. We were often reminded of these healthful habits in a martyred tone when we were having a treat or skipping breakfast. However, she acquired a taste for sweets as she aged. We discovered at a family picnic that she had eaten at least five desserts. Different people had offered her a taste of whatever dessert had just arrived without knowing she had already eaten several pieces of pie, cookies, and brownies. She enjoyed each offering without remembering the last.

My younger brother is a masterful potter and had a covered jar in the kitchen where they kept cookies for her. They could hear the lid clank as she helped herself to them during the day and evening. I remarked on one visit that the jar was one of the most beautiful he had ever made. My sister-in-law said it was funny about that pot; it did not sell when first made, so she took it to the house for a while, then back to the gallery several times. Since it had never gotten sold, she simply kept it in the house as a cookie jar for Mother.

Mother died a week before her ninety-fifth birthday and was cremated as she had desired. As we were all sitting around the table together discussing memorial service plans, my potter brother said that he wanted Mother's ashes to be buried in one of his pots. There was silence for a moment, then his wife said, "The cookie jar!"

On a beautiful day when all our family could gather from around the country and abroad, we held a memorial service for Mother. Her remains had been sealed into the cobalt blue pot, and it graced the service before it was lovingly carried to the cemetery plot to be buried next to our father.

A coincidence? No. I believe the "cookie jar" did not sell because it was Mother's pot. It brought beauty and sweetness into her daily life and now holds her ashes lovingly.

> *There, another cup done and set aside.*
> *Another relative to the ones gone before-*
> *something the first bequeathed to the most recent.*
> *And a silent chorus rising from them all:*
> *Everything, they remind us,*
> *used to be something else.*
> — Jack Troy, poet, potter, "Once, in Syracuse" from *Giving It Up to The Wind*

Tibetan Prayer Flags Meditation

Prayer flags originated in India and were incorporated into Tibetan Buddhist tradition.

Prayer flags are either rectangular or square and the color of each flag is linked to what it represents: blue (sky), white (air), red (fire), green (water) and yellow (earth). Tibetan prayer flags are bright and beautiful. All five colors together symbolize balance.

Tibetans believe the prayers and mantras attached to the flags will be spread by the wind and bring goodwill and positivity throughout the world. If you physically string flags, it's important to keep positive, selfless motivations in mind in keeping with the flags' ultimate purpose to promote peace, compassion, strength, healing, and wisdom to benefit all beings. Flags should be kept in good condition by replacing them as needed.

Intention: To expand your Heart Chakra to receive and send healing blessings of peace.

As you take relaxation breaths, ground by visualizing the soles of your feet attaching to the earth. Bring Light into your Crown Chakra from the center of the universe, filling your body with Light and clearing it of stress and tension. Center the Light in your Heart Chakra, which is expanding.

Visualize stringing a set of Tibetan prayer flags somewhere near you in a tree, out a window, on a roof, deck, or in your room. String them from left to right: blue, white, red, green, yellow. Imagine a world without violence and conflict. Place those images on your flags. Attach Compassion, Hope, Grace and Healing Light from your expanded Heart Chakra and let the wind blow them into the Universe for disbursement around the world, healing divisions, dispelling hate, and helping leaders make honorable and peaceful decisions. Leave your flags waving where you have placed them.

As you give thanks for this opportunity to send healing, consider what you can do to promote peace.

Take relaxation breaths and come back to the present with the assurance that your prayers, grace, compassion, and love are going into the world.

The secret to living well and longer: eat half, walk double, laugh triple, and love without measure.
— Tibetan Proverb

Indra's Net/Web Meditation

The story of Indra's Net first appears about 1000 BCE in the Athara Veda, one of four Vedic texts that form the foundation of the Hindu religion. In the story Indra was the leader of the Hindu pantheon of gods and was charged with the protection and guidance of humankind. Indra's Web is a vast net that stretches infinitely in all directions. In each "eye" of the net is a single brilliant, perfect jewel. Each jewel reflects every other jewel, and each of the reflected images bear the image of all the other jewels — infinity to infinity. When any jewel in the net is touched, all other jewels in the net are affected. Whatever affects one jewel affects them all. This speaks to the hidden interconnectedness and interdependency of everything and everyone in the Universe.

Intention: To become filled with Light, shining like a jewel and to send your Light to anyone in the world who needs it via Indra's Net.

Take relaxation breaths. Breathe normally as you picture yourself as a jewel. What jewel are you? What color? How large?
Bring Light from the Universe into your Crown Chakra

at the top of your head. As it gently flows through your body, clearing and grounding you, the Light turns the color of your jewel and you shine and glow.

Place your shining, jeweled self on Indra's Net that stretches over the world. How do you picture this web? Is it silver or gold, shiny, sparkly? Accept whatever image comes to you. You are connected to everyone in humanity with the threads of Indra's Web. You are taking Light where it is needed. Become increasingly quiet and still in the peace of this attachment. Stay in this space as long as you like.

Give thanks for the opportunity to help others via the Indra's Net/Web metaphor.

Take relaxation breaths and bring your attention back to the present.

> ***I live my life in widening circles***
> ***that reach out across the world.***
> — Rainer Maria Rilke

Passing Time Meditation

One hot summer day I was visiting my younger brother and his wife. She and I were sitting quietly on their porch, watching the creek flow by and not talking, simply being still together.

She suddenly turned to me and said, "The Africans called this Passing Time." Both were Peace Corps Africa (Sierra Leone) in the late 1960s.

I recently texted her to be sure I had the terminology and concept correct, and this is what she replied, "Yes indeed! 'Passing Time' it is. Often folks would drop by to visit and visiting meant being together, just sitting. Conversation wasn't necessary. If I was busy, I finished whatever I was doing and sat with them. There might be little talk but there was no issue with silence. It took some time to understand, and the best aspect: no guilt! There was no sense of intruding, no problem if I needed to complete my task; no need to fill airspace with idle chatter."

Intention: To sit Passing Time with yourself, using your breath to become quiet and calm.

As you take relaxation breaths, breathe in each of the

following words below. Repeat each word as you exhale, sending the meaning to your heart center. Breathe each word several times.

> Peace
> Calm
> Love
> Compassion
> Gratitude
> Courage
> Strength
> Hope

Add any words that come to mind as you do this.
Is there someone with whom you can sit Passing Time?
Give thanks as you take relaxation breaths.

Quiet the mind and the soul will speak.
— Ma Jaya Sati Bhagavati

Healing and Dying

One January, my husband and I traveled to Yorkshire, England to visit a couple with whom we had been friends for more than thirty-five years. Betty had been diagnosed with breast cancer several years prior to our visit, and she was thought to be in remission. We received word that the cancer had returned and was now metastatic. She was feeling tired but relatively well otherwise, and we wanted to spend time with both of them while we could still enjoy doing things together.

I had taken two levels of Healing Touch the previous July and September and was scheduled to take the third level in March, so I sent Betty a packet of information about the benefits of healing energy, what to expect in a session, and how energy travels through the body (blood, neurons, acupuncture meridians, etc.). When we arrived at their home, the first thing she said was, "I've been waiting for you." Betty stated that she had been searching for something spiritual and believed that Healing Touch was exactly what she had been looking for.

In the four days we were with our friends, Betty and I had a Healing Touch session daily. She said she felt more relaxed than she had ever felt in her life, and her energy had increased. I was able to teach her clearing, grounding, and chakra connection techniques, as well as simple visualization meditations that included breathing and setting Intentions for self-healing. At the end of one of the sessions she said that no matter what happened, her life had been wonderful and that she "had it all."

On our last morning together, shortly before we left for our flight home, in the middle of a storm of torrential rain and crashing wind, Betty and I sat across from each other at

~ Judith Stoddard ~

her kitchen table holding hands with closed eyes and sending unconditional love to each other. I heard her sobbing, looked up and was startled to see tears cascading down her face. She said that the love she felt coming into her was overwhelming. We decided that every Wednesday, at a given time, we would continue the practice of sending love to each other. When we said goodbye, we knew it was the last time we would all be together.

Betty died that May at age seventy. She was one of the loveliest women I will ever know. The day we learned of her death, I bought a half gallon of my favorite coffee ice cream and proceeded to eat it within twenty-hours, completely guilt-free and enjoying every wonderful spoonful. Doing this somehow felt like a tribute to her life and our long and important friendship. It was a reminder that we should value times together with people we love and care for each other and for ourselves in whatever way seems fitting. For me during this heartbreaking time it was eating coffee ice cream.

> *How careful we'd be if we kent [knew]*
> *which goodbyes were our last.*
> — Diana Gabaldon, *Outlander*

Silence of the Heart Meditation

Sometimes we find it difficult to communicate feelings using words. We may be so concerned with finding the right words to express ourselves that we miss the opportunity to experience the silence and grace that resides in our heart. When sitting quietly and concentrating on breathing we can create calming, heart-centered spaciousness.

Intention: To become aware of your heart and open it to receive its silence or messages.

Take relaxation breaths, breathing in the pure energy around you and breathing it into your heart center as you exhale. Your heart becomes calm as you do this.

As you continue to breathe slowly, picture your heart gently expanding and creating space for whatever feelings may arise.

Notice emotions you may have such as love, joy, happiness, fear, anger, grief, sadness. Acknowledge and accept feelings as you continue to breathe and focus on your heart, listening attentively to any messages you may be given.

Notice physical sensations like tightness, heaviness, or tenderness. Notice the rhythm of your heartbeat. Acknowledge and accept any sensations you have as you continue to breathe. If the sensations are uncomfortable, ask for them to be released.

Feelings are neither good nor bad. They just are.

Have any images or thoughts come to you during this meditation? If they have, you may want to journal them. Carrying beautiful images in your heart can help you stay in a calm space.

Our hearts are intuitive and understand how to care for us. Learn to listen to the heart's messages. As you create spaciousness in your heart, trust that you are being healed (made whole).

As you take relaxation breaths, give thanks for the opportunity to sit peacefully in awareness of your emotions and your heart.

Metta (Buddhist Loving Kindness Meditation)

May I be at Peace;
May my heart remain open;
May I awaken to the light of my own true nature;
May I be healed;
May I be a source of healing for all beings.

Judy's Heart Metta

May I hear my heart's silence;
May I understand it's intuitive messages;
May I be open to my heart's Gift of Grace;
May I share it with others.

Substitute "you" or a person's name for "I" in the Loving Kindness Metta, changing the other pronouns as needed. To send Grace, simply ask that it be sent from your Heart Center to another's.

~ Finding Peace ~

And in the stillness of your heart,
Your spirit can be unbound.
— Maya Angelou,
"The Power of Silence"

The Gift of Bruno

At age sixty-six, Bruno was diagnosed with pancreatic and liver cancer and given three months to live. I had learned of his diagnosis at a neighborhood party, and when I completed my first class of Healing Touch a month later I sent information to him on energy healing, inviting him for a session. His wife, Sue, called the following day to make an appointment for him, thus beginning our two-and-a-half-year journey together of love and hope, missing a weekly session only when one of us was out of town or had an unchangeable obligation.

This is Bruno's story, but it is also mine. I grew from a wide-eyed novice student of Healing Touch to a (still-awed) Certified Healing Touch Practitioner in those years, and Bruno was one of my most gifted teachers.

Bruno was retired from a thirty-five-year career as a chemical engineer. He had spent twenty-eight of those years as a navigator in the Air National Guard, where he met and married Sue, a flight nurse. Bruno's story is not about his disease process or his treatment with various chemotherapies, medical interventions, consultations, and exploration of possibly participating in clinical trials. It is the story of his inspiring trust, hope, sense of humor, and unwavering spirit of love.

From our first Healing Touch session, Bruno trusted. He put himself into God's hands through mine. He was interested in each new technique I learned and our standing joke upon my return from the next level class was that *now* I would get him levitated. In all sessions Bruno felt energy moving and went into deep relaxation mode, often sleeping soundly and seeing colors—varying shades and patterns of green and blue and often magenta and white. (The colors seen during Healing Touch sessions are usually colors of the chakras).

Our goals and healing intentions were to strengthen Bruno's immune system, increase efficacy of chemotherapy while decreasing its side effects, to attempt to contain his cancer, and Healing for his Highest Good, an energetic term referring to turning the healing over to a Higher Power. He was able to travel to Hawaii several times to see grandchildren, to play golf almost weekly, go to baseball games, lunch with friends, and enjoy family gatherings. He attended church regularly. Bruno was sometimes tired, but until his last few months lived an active life with minimal chemotherapy side effects and pain. Sue learned basic Healing Touch techniques to do with him when they were away. During those times I did long-distance healing and experienced seeing patterns of greens and blues as I visualized sending healing energy to him.

The Healing Touch sessions in Bruno's hospice bed were shorter than usual. He had given me a Tibetan singing bowl and I always made it *sing* at the end of each session with him. He smilingly said it was his insurance that the session "took." I carried it with me to his home those last weeks, and as I ended a session the day before he died, I told him that he was "tuned up." Bruno gave me his quiet smile and, as always, a hug. Even as Bruno's health deteriorated, our goals and intentions never wavered. I believe they were met.

The next morning I received a call that Bruno had unexpectedly declined during the night, and family and friends were gathering. I was asked to come. His daughter and I held his feet as he died, opening the chakras in the soles of his feet and feeling great warmth come into them. He was surrounded by people he loved and who loved him. Bruno was a pure example of holism. He was a man of faith, had wonderful support from family and friends, excellent medical care, and most importantly, he never lost hope. His courage was an inspiration to everyone who knew him and to some who did not. He will be immeasurably missed.

Bruno gave me many gifts, but his incomparable gift was the understanding of what being "heart-centered" truly means—not the book or class definition but the reality of actually *feeling* love and compassion pouring out of my Heart Center into another person while doing Healing Touch. And for that gift I will be forever thankful.

I Want Blue!

I'm living in "The Time of Lasts." Sometimes I wonder if what I am doing or where I am going will be the last time I have the opportunity to do or see it. People are continually writing about aging, which, quite frankly, I didn't fully understand until I entered this Time of Lasts.

For years a friend of mine has driven a Tahoe. She always buys a light blue one. The old one she had seemed to be telling her that it was going to need significant repairs to remain dependable, and she felt it was time to trade it in for a new model.

She went to the dealer and explained exactly what she wanted, including the color: light blue. He said that they had a black one on the lot that she could drive home that day. She said, "I want blue." He went on a computer and told her that there was a white Tahoe at a dealer in the next town, and they could have it ready for pickup the next day. She said, "I want blue." He again went on the computer and told her the only one he could find was in the Midwest, but it would take at least a week to get it to their dealership. She leaned across the desk toward him and replied, "This is my last car, and I want blue!"

My mother belonged to a bridge club which rotated monthly between the members' homes. These lifelong friends went through bearing and raising children, family problems, and losing husbands together. They began to call themselves The Widows Club until one by one they themselves became ill and died. My mother was the last one standing in that group, one week away from turning ninety-five. My brothers and I had known these women all our lives, and I felt sad as they each left the circle, but I had moved away and could be supportive only from a distance. I didn't understand the depth of these losses to my mother, but now I'm beginning to.

I have a cadre of friends who are widows, and one recently widowed woman said that the loss can't be understood until you go through it. I'm sure this is as true as it was for me trying to understand the pain my mother felt when losing her friends. And especially when she lost my father.

I used to smile at my Aunt Marion, who put our names on special family belongings that she wanted us to have or gave them to us on birthdays to be sure we had them. I am doing the same thing, as well as making a list of "who gets what" for our children and grandchildren.

This Time of Lasts has a feeling of turning things over to others, an awareness of pulling back, of minor and major losses, of greater fatigue and potential health concerns.

There is an urgency about staying in touch with family and friends, of telling the stories, sharing memories, of remembering the fun times and laughter. There is urgency about getting things in order and of getting rid of things not needed so adult children won't have to deal with them. There is a feeling of wondering what's next, and when. And who.

The Time of Lasts is also a time of permitting minor self-indulgences, of needing little, of increased generosity, and of enhanced appreciations and enjoyments.

Blessings abound. My heart overflows with love. These will be *always* never *lasts*.

I'm living in The Time of Lasts . . . and I want blue!

Fifth Chakra (Throat)

Truthfulness
Self-Expression
Communication
Choice

Location: Base of Throat

Color: Blue

Element: Sound and Space

Anatomy: Throat, Thyroid, Tongue, Lips, Cheeks, Jaws, Teeth, Ears

Open (Balanced): Ability to Speak One's Truth, Clear Communication, Peace, Mercy

Blocked (Compromised): Physical Problems Affecting Head Below the Eyes, Mouth, Sore Throat, Laryngitis, Neck Issues, Dizziness, Lack of Connection With One's Purpose or Vocation, Inappropriate Speech, Gossip

Affirmations:

I speak my truth honestly and clearly.
I listen and hear others.
I am faithful and loyal.
I maintain appropriate silences.
I make excellent choices.
I sing well.
I am peaceful

Words Matter Meditation

When your Heart is open to possibilities, you start to notice small things that can lead to enormous discoveries.
— Masaru Emoto
The Hidden Messages in Water

In his research, Masaru Emoto, a Japanese scientist, discovered that molecules of water are affected by our thoughts, words, and feelings. He infused water with positive and negative words, finding that water crystals became either beautiful or misshapen depending on the words that were used. The most beautiful crystals were formed by using the words Love and Gratitude. Since humans are mainly composed of water and 70% of the Earth is covered by water, words matter.

Intention: To be empowered and inspired by the following positive, supportive words.

As you take relaxation breaths, connect with your Inner Self by guiding the breath into the Heart Chakra.
From your Third Eye, Sixth Chakra at your brow, open

~ Finding Peace ~

yourself to the magic and gifts of the Universe that will be brought to you today through words. Through this portal, you find yourself standing or sitting at the edge of a lovely pool. You see words falling from the heavens. As you watch, you realize they have different shapes and forms. Some words gently slip into the water while others splash as they enter.

The word **Gratitude** is filled with many natural things: flowers, birds, trees, animals, and people of all cultures. It slowly floats down and enters the pool.

The word **Laughter** noisily does summersaults until it reaches the water and rollickingly enters with a happy splash.

The word **Fun** is riding a bicycle and rides in circles in the air as it falls, then rides around on top of the water of the pool before it enters in a rush with a smiling face.

The words **Courage**, **Strength**, and **Honesty** are attached to eagle feathers and twirl as they fall, making small whirlpools in the water as they sink.

The word **Peace** is carried by doves and is placed softly into the water.

The word **Cosmos** is made of stars, Sun, and Moon and is shaped into the symbol for infinity. The water glows and shimmers as it enters.

The word **Prayer** drops in feet first with the arms of its **Y** raised toward the heavens.

The word **Hope** changes into shapes that are used to represent it as it falls . . . a butterfly, a rainbow, a seedling, a sunrise followed by a sunset.

The word **Love** falls last. It is a widening, never-ending circle that encompasses all.

Imagine drinking cool water from your pool and allowing these words to heal all the cells in your body.

There are many other positive words that want to be in your life. Do any come to you now? What shapes might they take?

~ Judith Stoddard ~

Take relaxation breaths as you give thanks for the power of words.

Guide my thoughts before they become my words.
— Rev. Roy Ressin
"Prayer Before You Speak"

Lunchbox Notes

When our children were small and carrying lunches to school, I often put notes into their lunch boxes that said things like, "Hi!" or "I love you" or "Eat your spinach," knowing that they considered spinach an adversarial vegetable and, of course, I hadn't packed any for them. I included stick figures or funny sayings to make them smile. Sometimes they told me a bit huffily that other moms didn't leave notes with cookies or sandwiches, and I replied that I wasn't just *anybody's* Mom. When they did the "Oh, Mom" sigh, they attempted to hide small smiles. They liked getting the notes, and I liked writing them. The notes seemed like little security blankets to help the children get through the school day.

I recently bought a secondhand book online relating to wholeness and healing. The book's previous owner had left little tabs of paper and cardboard corner markers throughout the book. It was as though I was being encouraged to take special note of what was written on those pages. The markers felt like lunchbox notes even though nothing was written on them, and they weren't from my departed mother. I did pay closer attention to the paragraphs and pages that were marked.

A good friend creates sacred areas around her home with favorite objects that may not have significance to anyone else. I have started making such spaces on kitchen ledges, around my computer, and on my bureau. The items placed there serve as reminders of what is important to me . . . family and friends here and gone, happy times, gifts from nature, and remembered places. Some of them are simply silly. All are miniature lunchbox notes to myself, and I am happy to receive them.

Insights on Waiting

Paraphrased dictionary definitions of "waiting": To stay where one is or delay action until a particular time or until something else occurs. It may indicate that one is eagerly impatient to do something or for something to happen.

Sometimes we:
> Wait for babies to be born. Wait as a loved one is dying.
> Wait for a reply to a job or college application. Wait for a project or education to be completed.
> Wait for a diagnosis to be made, treatment to be finished, and a return to sound health.
> Wait to find the right partner or for relationships to end.

During the Covid pandemic we:
> Waited for researchers to understand the virus and for a vaccine to be developed.
> Waited for schools to resume sessions.
> Waited for travel to be safe.
> Waited for a time when people could gather for graduations, wedding ceremonies, parties, and for usual activities to resume.

Add personal insights on waiting that you may have.

As we wait, the challenge is to try to stay patient and discern and understand what personal growth we are experiencing, growth that may not have occurred otherwise. The challenge is to be kind to ourselves while we wait.

Sun Power Meditation

Our solar system, with the Sun in the center, was formed more than 4.5 billion years ago. The Sun is Earth's star with a radius of more than one hundred times the radius of the Earth and was named Helios by the ancient Greeks and Sol by the Romans. While the Sun takes up 99.8 percent of the mass in our solar system, it is considered small in comparison to suns in most other solar systems. The Sun is considered a masculine energy. Its true color is white, and it takes solar energy approximately 8.3 minutes to reach Earth from the Sun. Its ultraviolet light triggers the production of endorphins, the "feel good" hormones that relieve pain, reduce stress, and improve mood. Its UV light synthetizes into vitamin D, which is crucial for bone health and aids in strengthening the immune system.

Intention: To explore how you can utilize the chakra system's qualities while receiving the healing light of the Sun. To affirm your strengths by speaking them aloud.

Take gentle relaxation breaths, feeling tension leaving your body with each exhalation.
Visualize yourself sitting or lying in the sunlight—at the

beach, on a grassy knoll, on your deck, or in your back yard; wherever you love to be. It is that first day of late spring when the sun is strong, something you have been waiting for during the winter.

The sun's healing rays are coming into each chakra. You may see their colors in your mind's eye.

First Chakra (Root; color red) – Consider your family, clan, and tribe (includes friends and groups). How can you support them holistically: physically, emotionally, mentally, and spiritually? Ask for the Sun's power to strengthen these connections. Affirm: My energy and life force are strong.

Second Chakra (Sacral; color orange) – Consider ways you are creative, joyful, and enthusiastic. How could you use the Sun to support these in your life? Affirm: I love life!

Third Chakra (Solar Plexus color yellow) – Consider how you are courageous. How do you manage situations when you are feeling less than confident? In what ways are you determined? How do you make decisions to move forward? How can the Sun help? Affirm: I am trusting and strong.

Fourth Chakra (Heart; green) – Consider how you express love and compassion. Are you grieving (loss of people, pets, physical or mental abilities, homes, something else)? Do you need to forgive someone? Yourself? How can you open your heart to the Sun's warmth? Affirm: I can give and receive love and express emotions in a safe way.

Fifth Chakra (Throat; blue) – Consider how you speak your truth at appropriate times. Do you communicate clearly? Are you an active listener? Can the Sun help with these traits? Affirm: I can remain peaceful as I speak and listen.

Sixth Chakra (Brow; indigo purple, blue) – Consider how you visualize. Can you visualize? If not, are there ways you could develop doing so? In what ways are you wise? Perceptive? What could you do to enhance these gifts? The Sun may help with keeping this chakra open. Affirm: I am intelligent, intuitive, and open to insights.

Seventh Chakra (Crown; white, orchid, lavender, purple) – Consider the ways in which you are spiritual. How do you feel connected to whatever Higher Power is meaningful to you? The Sun reaches to the divine. Affirm: I can trust my Higher Self, my Inner Teacher, and I am connected to the Divine.

As you take relaxation breaths, give thanks for the healing energy of the Sun and for opportunities to share your individual gifts.

> *The sun, with all those planets revolving around it and dependent on it, can still ripen a bunch of grapes as if it had nothing else in the universe to do.*
> — Galileo Galilei

Armadillo Lessons

The armadillo has much to teach us about protection and setting boundaries. When feeling threatened it rolls itself into a ball and uses its natural armor to set boundaries that cannot be penetrated.

We may feel in need of physical or energetic protection when in the presence of someone whose energy feels dark and heavy, or in an emotionally charged environment when we want to block negativity from entering our biofield. We may wish for protection when entering a hospital, being with someone who is ill, when driving in dangerous traffic or in severe weather conditions, or in a myriad of other difficult situations.

At such times it may be helpful to use a mental protective visualization such as placing oneself in a bubble, circle, or column of pure white light or dropping a finely meshed jeweled net over yourself to block unwanted thoughts or emotions from entering your energy field, while allowing your Light and positive energy to shine through. Armadillo's shield placed in front of you can be a safeguard. Personal protective images may come to mind.

In situations where you feel vulnerable, it is beneficial to stay grounded and centered and to set your own boundaries. Defining your space helps to keep a balance between you and the person or situation. Asking for help in what I call "one-liners" (prayers) such as "Please keep me safe" or simply, "I need help" may offer reassurance that you are not alone.

And always give thanks when the issue is safely resolved.

Don't take on anything that doesn't belong to you.
— Judith Stoddard

Journaling for Clarity

Journaling is one way of manifesting desires, being in the moment, and reaching your Inner Teacher/Intuition for healing and clarity.

During Level One class of Healing Touch, it was suggested that we begin journaling if we were not already doing so. I didn't begin. It was again suggested in Levels Two and Three; still, I didn't begin. In Level Four class, the importance of journaling for practitioners was firmly stressed.

The class was held at a retreat center in the mountains of Arizona. I was with a friend who had been journaling for years, and I mentioned that I simply didn't see myself journaling no matter how important it was. She asked, "Why? Because you think someone will read it after you're dead?" I replied that that was part of it, to which she said emphatically, "So what? You're dead!"

When I finally started journaling, my husband gave me a beautiful red leather journal for Valentine's Day. It was too small to use for journaling, so I use it for special thoughts. A friend also gave me a beautiful leather-bound, medium-sized journal. It was still too small. I use it to save unique quotes or sayings. I journal in an 8 X 10 lined spiral notebook with a welcoming cover. I have found that this is just right for me because it allows for unrestrained writing. I have full confidence that no one will invade my privacy by reading what I journal, but I affix a label on the front in red lettering that says, *You do not have permission to read this journal[signed] Mom/Judy* in case it is . . . well, found after I'm dead.

There is no right or wrong way to journal, no judgement, and no concern with quality of handwriting. Writing quickly and honestly is helpful. A journal can be a good friend with whom you share secrets or tell innermost thoughts, concerns, and emotions. I have written blistering, angry comments, and the paper has yet to catch fire. Some pages have tear drop blots. Most often I journal mornings, but any convenient time is fine. I reach for it during the day if I have an experience I want to hold onto, so I don't forget the details. I may journal every day for a long stretch and then weeks pass without journaling. I seem to go in fits and starts. Often I sit down to journal and begin by writing that I don't have anything to say and continue writing until several pages are filled. I place the date and time on each page as I begin.

Because journaling serves me best by using it as an in-the-moment reflective tool, I don't reread the notebooks. Solutions to a problem may become clear as I journal, or creative ideas are born. Journaling may jog thoughts that continue to bubble up as the day or week evolves. Others find that reading their journals after a lapse of time provides details of an experience they want to remember or to denote growth. Reviewing a journal may be particularly helpful after a period of grief to help recognize progress in healing. While experiencing the meditations or stories in this book, personal images or thoughts may arise. Journaling paragraphs or simply jotting down reminder words may be valuable tools for reflection. If journaling is new for you and you don't have a journal on hand, I encourage you to consider getting one that is exactly right for you.

Psychiatrists, psychologists, and researchers have proposed that there are mental and physical benefits to journaling, particularly when writing by hand rather than on a computer. They suggest that journaling increases brain connectivity, engages sensory and motor processing areas and regions associated with memory, boosts cognitive skills and the immune system response, decreases anxiety and stress, magnifies gratitude, and stimulates creativity.

All I know is that I always feel better when I journal.

All Shall Be Well Affirmations Meditation

*All shall be well,
and all shall be well,
and all manner of thing
shall be well,*

*For there is a force of love
moving through The Universe
that holds us fast and
never lets us go.*
— Julian of Norwich

Affirmations are positive statements that help you to challenge and overcome self-doubt and negative thoughts. *Believing* and repeating them often can facilitate positive changes. Empirical studies show that self-affirmations may mitigate the effects of stress.

Intention: To relieve stress and fear. To instill confidence.

Take relaxation breaths. Repeat each affirmation as needed. Place your hand on your Solar Plexus Chakra (stomach) as you say aloud:

- Although I am anxious about our country's and the world's divisions, I am strong. I know that "All shall be well" and let go of my anxiety.
- Although I fear that I have no control about what is happening around me, I am courageous and let go of my fear.
- Although my stress level may be high, I trust that "there is a force of love moving through the Universe that holds us fast and never lets us go." I let go of my stress.
- Although I sometimes feel helpless, I remain confident in my strengths. I let go of my feeling of helplessness.
- Although I may be apprehensive, I remain self-assured. I let go of my apprehension.
- Although I get worried, I try to remain calm. I let go of my worry.
- Although I forget that I can control my breathing, I consciously slow it now.
- I truly believe that all shall be well. I give thanks for my strengths and gifts.

Trust and Go Forward.
— A Scottish Clan Urquhart Motto

Sixth Chakra (Brow; Third Eye)

Intuition
Foresight
Vision

Location: Behind Forehead, Between Eyes

Color: Indigo Purple

Element: Wind or Air

Anatomy: Pituitary gland, Lymph, Eyes, Sinuses, Upper Head

Open (Balanced): Wisdom, Visualization, Mystery, Faith, Loyalty, Inspiration, Mind, Intellect, Perception

Blocked (Compromised): Eye Strain, Tension and Migraine Headaches, Dizziness, Blocked Sinuses, Hearing and Memory Issues, Insomnia, Sensitivity to Light

Affirmations:

I visualize well.
I am often inspired.
I am generous and think positively.
I have dynamic thoughts and energy.
My intellect and perception are keen.

Floating Meditation

Floating in water can heal by providing a physically supportive and mentally soothing therapeutic environment. The Sixth Chakra (the Third Eye), located on the forehead between the eyebrows is the center of intuition, foresight, openness, and imagination. This meditation provides an opportunity to combine the relaxation of floating with receiving intuitive gifts.

Intention: To become relaxed and open to the magic of the Universe and the intuitive gifts it may bring to you today.

Place your hand on your forehead as you take relaxation breaths, breathing in the pure energy around you and expanding your Sixth Chakra on exhalation.

Through this portal, find yourself by the mystical lake of Avalon, or by the sea or body of water of your choosing—whatever comes to you. The water is crystal clear and very blue, and it may be shallow or deep. The bottom is sandy.

The day is peaceful and quiet. No one is around. You are comfortable being alone and are dressed in light, gauzy, white or pastel-colored clothing. Your feet are unencumbered by shoes.

~ Finding Peace ~

As you approach the water and begin to wade into it, you are relaxed and unafraid. Even if you can't swim or feel uneasy in water, you know you will be safe, buoyant, and supported. The water is soft. If you are in the ocean, the waves lap tenderly as you rise and fall in their swell. If you are in a natural pool or lake, the water is still.

Slowly turn around and lie down in the water, arms outstretched, floating without effort. If you are in a natural pool, float to the middle. If you are in the ocean or bay, float a short distance from shore. Your eyes are closed and your hair may be floating around you.

Because your ears are in the water, you don't hear external sounds but hear your heart beating steadily and strongly, reminiscent of listening to your mother's comforting and reassuring heartbeat while floating in amnionic fluid.

As you rest in the water, any concerns, pain, grief, problems, or stress slowly drop away from you and sink.

Hundreds of tiny, star-like bioluminescent phytoplankton scintillate and surround you like a starry sky as you float. Welcome these beautiful colored points of light that bring healing, joy, and gratitude as they touch you. Your favorite flower may be floating around you. You feel happy, as though you could stay here forever, simply floating.

Remember a time when you consciously followed your intuition and had a positive outcome. What were the circumstances? How did this outcome influence your life or someone else's life? Give thanks for following and trusting the gifts of your Third Eye.

Was there a time when you neglected to follow your intuition and should have done so? Was there a time you followed it and later felt it was not the correct decision? Were there negative outcomes or missed opportunities because of these decisions? If you felt regretful or are still feeling regretful about a result, release it and let it float away. Regret is not serving you.

Are you receiving insights or imaginative gifts from your intuition as you float? If so, how can you implement them? Consider writing them in your journal. If nothing is noted, simply enjoy floating peacefully. Frequently insights and ideas come at unexpected times, in unexpected ways, in unexpected places or by unexpected people after meditating. Remain open to the possibility of receiving intuitive gifts.

When it is time to leave, float to the edge of your body of water. Drop your feet to the bottom, stand and slowly walk to the shore. As you lie down on the warm sandy beach, you discover you are miraculously dry and back in your clothes. You are rested and energized.

This place is yours alone and you may come back anytime you would like to receive these cleansing, creative, and intuitive Gifts of Spirit.

As you take relaxation breaths, give thanks for this peaceful float .

> *Deep peace of the running wave to you.*
> *Deep peace of the flowing air to you.*
> *Deep peace of the quiet earth to you.*
> *Deep peace of the shining stars to you.*
> *Deep peace of the infinite peace to you.*
>   (Adapted from ancient Gaelic runes)

Intuition Quotes: Sixth and Third Chakra Differences

The Sixth Chakra (Forehead, "Third Eye;" Imagination/Wisdom) is the center of intuition and foresight. Intuition is defined as an ability to understand or know something instinctively and immediately based on feelings, openness, and imagination rather than conscious reasoning and facts. Intuitions are generated by unconscious "pattern matching" of the mind rapidly sifting through past experiences and cumulative knowledge delivered to current awareness with considerable emotional certainty.

Intuition is different from the Third Chakra's Gut Feeling/Instinct which is defined as a physical manifestation of our intuition (examples: muscle tightness, goose bumps, uneasy feeling of nausea, butterflies in stomach, sweaty palms). Gut instinct does what is necessary to keep us safe and alive (flight, fight, or freeze). Gut instinct is not as dependable a guide to building innovative processes in creative thinking as Intuition.

Instinct and Gut Feeling frequently work together and the words are often interchanged and paired.

Intuition Quotes:

The intuitive mind is a sacred gift and the rational mind is a faithful servant. We have created society that honors the servant and has forgotten the gift. The only real valuable thing is intuition.
— Albert Einstein

Listen to the wind, it talks. Listen to the silence, it speaks. Listen to your heart, it knows.
— Native American Proverb

~ Judith Stoddard ~

Have the courage to follow your heart and intuition. They somehow already know what you truly want to become. Everything else is secondary.
— Steve Jobs

Intuition is seeing with the soul.
— Dean Koontz

Anonymous Quotes:

Intuition is real. Vibes are real. Energy doesn't lie. Tune in.

There is a voice that doesn't use words. Listen.

You know the truth by the way it feels.

Trust your instincts. Intuition doesn't lie. When it is roaring loudly follow it.

Your first instinct is usually right. You feel before you think.

Deep down you already know the truth.

Candle Gazing
A Preparation for Meditation

Candle Gazing (Taraka) is an ancient meditation practice. According to some spiritual traditions, Candle Gazing activates the Brow Chakra (sixth energy center, our Third Eye) that is associated with insight, intuition, and higher consciousness by creating a feedback loop to the pineal gland that secretes melatonin, a sleep-promoting hormone. This gland controls other hormones as well.

It is thought that this gazing offers the benefits of improved concentration and focus, reduces stress, enhances vision, promotes better sleep, and removes negative thoughts, promoting mental clarity. While this is a safe practice for almost anyone, it is recommended that those with epilepsy choose something steady at which to gaze rather than a flickering flame. It should not be used with anyone suffering from headaches or migraines as it may aggravate them.

Candle gazing is a way to prepare for meditating.

Sit quietly in a quiet place.

Put your candle on a steady surface 3–4 feet in front of you. Light the candle. A highly scented candle may be distracting.

Focus on the flame for 1–2 minutes and gaze steadily. Try to avoid blinking for as long as possible.

~ Judith Stoddard ~

Close your eyes and try to visualize the flame being at your Third Eye between your eyebrows. Hold the image until it begins to fade.

Open your eyes and repeat the process several times.

Blow out the candle. Begin meditating as the smoke rises.

An LED candle may be used if you prefer not using a lighted candle.

Back to Basics: A Meditation Template

Sometimes a devastating situation arises for which we have no words. Any number of life occurrences such as loss of a loved one, a family crisis, frightening health diagnosis, divorce, or world situation may initiate this feeling. During such times, the techniques we use daily to stay centered, calm, and balanced may feel ineffective. This meditation template is designed for such times. Personalize it to address the circumstance. Feel free to insert Intentions, techniques, poems, and prayers from other meditations to tailor this template to your current needs.

Meditation Position: Sit or lie quietly in an area where you won't be disturbed or distracted. If in a chair, sit erect with a straight spine, relaxed shoulders, neck, and facial muscles, hands resting gently in your lap. Tilting your chin slightly downward may help hold your position. Place your feet flat on the floor with or without shoes. If lying down, use pillows to support your head, shoulders, and knees. If walking, do it mindfully. Ground yourself.

Breathe: Concentrate on breathing. It has been said that Spirit whispers to us between breaths. Be aware of the lungs filling, releasing, and slowing. It is the mind's job to think. If thoughts arise, acknowledge them and then let them float away. Address important thoughts after you finish meditating.

Set an Intention: Ask for help, strength, stress relief, or whatever request you have during this time. You can simply say, "I need help" or "This is overwhelming." State your feelings, own them, and request support. Turn it over to Spirit.

~ Judith Stoddard ~

Open Yourself: Express openness to receiving help. Suggestions on how to do this are to revisit a formerly used meditation, journal your feelings, randomly open a book of poems, blessings, or inspirations, or the Bible or other devotional book and read the page's message. You are welcome to do this several times using different sources. Listen for a message in a favorite piece of music or song. Be aware of thoughts or images that come to you from nature or other sources during these practices. Visualize being filled with Healing Light and having it surround you.

Affirmations: Read or write affirmations to strengthen you and instill courage and hope.

Give Thanks: Even in dire circumstances there are opportunities to express thanks. Make a mental or written gratitude list to help allay anxieties and concerns. Postpone this activity if it is too difficult to do in the current situation.

To end, concentrate on your breathing as you continue to sit quietly.

Any of these tools can be used individually throughout the day.

Trust the timing of your life.
— Brittany Burgunder

Spirit Wind Meditation

The word spirit in Hebrew and Greek means breath or wind. Spirit is the vital breath of the Universe. The wind represents the power of Sprit in sustaining life and holding it together. It has a symbolic association with the words cord, rope, and thread. Spirit is sometimes pictured as such. Energetic Cords tie us together. We breathe unconsciously and take our respirations for granted. It has been said that sometimes the wind speaks to us in whispers between breaths. Wind is the element for the Sixth Chakra (Brow/Intuition), while breath is the Fourth Chakra, Heart. Their characteristics are combined in this meditation.

Intention: To become aware of breathing and appreciate the wind's teachings.

As you take relaxation breaths, concentrate on your breathing. What happens physically when you breathe? Take belly breaths, sending the breath to the abdomen so it rises. Change to more rapid breathing as if you had just walked rapidly or up a hill or a flight of stairs. Go back to deeper, slower, more even breaths. Hold your breath for four seconds on intake; pause; slowly exhale and hold it again for four seconds. Pause. Do this for several breaths. Go back to gentle, regular breathing.

Consider and Give Thanks for:
The freshness the breath brings into your body; the life force known as Qi (chi).

The purity of wholeness and health that air gives you, aerating your blood, which in turn provides nourishing oxygen to all cells and organs in your body. The lungs filter environmental impurities that we breathe in every day.

The strength that the breath/wind often symbolizes: the power to overcome obstacles. Bring this strength into yourself.

The Wind Teaches Us:
How to persevere in storms. Are you utilizing this attribute in your current life situation?

That it is independent of us. What can this aspect of independence teach you?

To be whimsical and playful. How can you incorporate these into your daily life?

That it can be soft, nurturing, and reassuring. How and where can you apply these qualities?

Sometimes the wind is destructive and very forceful, characteristics best left uncultivated.

Visualize the wind blowing through you and around your body and energy field. Is it warm or cold? Strong, tumultuous, gentle, forceful, directive, calming? Does it bring a message? Sit quietly and ask if it does. However Spirit Wind comes to you, know that it is cleansing, grounding, and restoring you.

Send Spirit Wind's traits and the purity of your breath and energy field to people who are important in your life, to situations and places in need of cleansing, and into the atmosphere. Give thanks as you take relaxation breaths.

> **When the winds of change blow, some people build walls and others build windmills.**
> — Chinese proverb

Thin Places Meditation

There is a Celtic saying that heaven and earth are only three feet apart, but in the thin places, that distance is even smaller (thinner). Thin places are where the veil between the worlds lifts and Spirit is experienced more directly. Examples of natural Thin Places are Stonehenge in England, Sedona in Arizona, the Giza Pyramid in Egypt, Machu Picchu in Peru, and Iona in Scotland.

Iona beaches are filled with beautiful ancient boulders, rocks, stones, crystals, and pebbles displaying a vast range of colors and textures. It is believed that the ancient crystalline nature of the rocks contributes immeasurably to the special and unique feelings of joy, peace, rejuvenation, and wonderment that emanate across the island. Any place where hearts are open and the sacred becomes present to us can be a thin place. They are refuges.

Intention: To enter a Sacred Space and receive deep relaxation, calmness, healing, or specific gifts you are asking Spirit to bring to you.

As you take relaxation breaths, bring peaceful words into your mind.

~ Finding Peace ~

Geological Thin Places – If you have been to a Thin Place, remember where it was and how you felt while there. Did you have a feeling of being in a holy place? If you have not visited one, imagine being on the Scottish island of Iona with the clear blue-green sea before you and the extraordinary stones underfoot and boulders surrounding you. Be open to thoughts or images that may come to you while visualizing being in these spaces.

Desert – Envision yourself sitting alone in the desert at sunrise. It is cool and quiet. It feels spacious. All you can see are sand dunes and the Sun slowly coming over the horizon. Are you being given insights or images? How do you feel?

Woods – Imagine walking deep into the woods to your mother tree. Rest on the earth with your back against her trunk. Is there a message for you today? If another type of tree comes to you, she is bringing a message. Messages can simply be feelings you receive, such as becoming still or strong.

Your home – Is there a place you have made sacred or can call your own? Sometimes favorite items gravitate to this area. A yard, garden, deck, or porch can become a Thin Place. Anywhere is a sacred space if you think of it as such.

Give thanks for the awareness of Thin Places and for your blessings. Name them. Ask for personal help if needed and help for those in your life who need your care and concern. Ask for help for all who are hurting in the world and help for our struggling planet. Take relaxation breaths and return to the present.

~ Judith Stoddard ~

"Thin places," the Celts call this space,
both seen and unseen,
where the door between the world
and the next is cracked open for a moment
and the light is not all on the other side.
God-shaped space.
— Sharlande Sledge

Seventh Chakra (Crown)

Intuition
Foresight
Vision

Location: Slightly above Center of Top of Head

Color: Bright White and Golden Light, Violet

Element: Pure Light, Thought

Anatomy: Brain, Hypothalamus and Pineal Glands

Open (Balanced): Spirituality, Connection to Higher Self, Enlightenment, Dynamic Thought and Energy, Consciousness, Inner Peace, Unity, Clarity

Blocked (Compromised): Feeling Disconnected from Spirit, Inability to Make Simple Decisions, Dissociation, Depression, Perceived Loss of Connection to Soul

Affirmations:

I am spiritual.
I trust my Higher Self, my Inner Teacher.
I am connected to the Divine Wisdom of the universe.
I am wise.
I am self-aware.

Light

Light is one of the most universal and fundamental symbols. It is not just the absence of darkness; it is the spiritual and the divine, illumination, intelligence, knowledge, wisdom, vision, goodness, and insight. World religions often utilize the analogy of light to speak of a divine presence, both in human life and in eternity. Light communicates through spiritual means as well as physical means. In theology, Divine Light is also called Divine Radiance or Divine Refulgence (to shine). The energy of Divine Light is the spiritual force that is present and that activates all things. This Light is in everything, every aspect of our experience and our expression.

Light is the pure energy of Spirit that encompasses all levels of consciousness and is available for use. To receive Healing Light, simply ask for its presence to come, for example, "I ask for Light to fill, clear, surround, and protect me." You may use similar words. It is the Intention that is important. Send Light to others using the Crown Chakra.

Light Quotes:

> *You are the Light of the World.*
> *Your Light must shine for all.*
> — Matthew 5:14.16

Darkness cannot drive out darkness: only light can do that.
— Martin Luther King, Jr.

> *Some days you will be a light for others,*
> *and some days you will need a light from them.*
> *As long as there is light there is hope.*
> — Jennifer Gayle

~ Finding Peace ~

Nothing can dim the light that shines from within.
— Maya Angelou

The greater the Light in our lives, the fewer the shadows.
— Ian S. Ardern

*Shine your Light into the world and
even if that's all you ever do, that is enough.*
— Unknown

*You're not here to bring Light into the world.
You're here to Be Light.*
— Abraham Hicks

*The more light you allow within you,
the brighter the world you live in will be.*
— Shakti Gawain

Sometimes our light goes out but is blown again into instant flame by an encounter with another human being.
— Dr. Albert Schweitzer

*There is a crack in everything God has made.
That's how the light gets in.*
— Ralph Waldo Emerson

*Turn your face to the sun and
the shadows will fall behind you.*
— Māori proverb

Lighthouses don't go running all over an island looking for boats to save; they just stand there shining.
— Anne Lamott

The Light within me honors the Light within you. Namaste.
(one interpretation)
— Unknown Author

Spaciousness Meditation

Quantum physics verifies the scientific, biological fact that one percent of every atom that makes up the human body is composed of protons, neutrons, and electrons. The other ninety-nine percent is empty space. Spaciousness of our mind and heart allows us to be open to positive emotions and be in the present. It helps us let go of negative thoughts, feelings, and judgement.

Intention: To allow your mind and heart to open and become spacious. As you take relaxation breaths, breathe in the pure energy around you. Let go of stress and any negative thoughts on exhalation, making it twice as long as inhalation. Breathe gently as you rest in present moment awareness. Once you are still, your Qi, your life force, begins to move and flow.

Become aware of the room you are in. Notice the objects that are around you. Are there any favorite pieces? Why are they meaningful to you? Do they carry a message? A special memory?

Notice the space in the room. It is peaceful and calm. The room may feel as though it is limited by walls, but space

~ Finding Peace ~

is unlimited. The space around all of us is the same. It is one way for us to be connected to each other and to all of life.

Send the breath to your Heart Center. With each breath, expand your heart, clearing away tension and stress in all parts of your body.

Send the breath to your mind and Crown Chakra. Acknowledge any thoughts that arise and let them dissipate and float away. If a thought arises that you need to address, come back to it later. You are giving your mind a rest. It is quiet.

Your heart and mind expansion continues into the infinite space of the Universe that holds such mystery, beauty, and love. You are in a spaciousness that knows no bounds and allows all good things to enter such as kindness, compassion, love, healing, gratitude, peace, joy, and hope.

The Universe is the whole of us. Bring light images of distant galaxies to mind as recorded by the Hubble and Webb telescopes.

Rest in this spaciousness as you give thanks for the opportunity to expand your heart and mind. Bring your awareness back to the present with a few letting-go breaths.

I am larger, better than I thought;
I did not know I held so much goodness.
— Walt Whitman

Ribbons of Grace and Light Meditation

Grace is prayer, thanksgiving, and blessing. Synonyms: benevolence, favor, goodness, goodwill, elegance, poise, ease, refinement, gracefulness.

Intention: To receive and share Grace and Light.

Take relaxation breaths, sinking into a state of Spirit-centered quiet with each breath. Breathe quietly throughout the meditation.

Picture divine, colored healing ribbons full of Grace and Light softly floating down onto you, over, and around you. What is their source? Are they anchored in the stars, dropped by Light Beings, coming from the Sun, from shooting stars or simply falling free from an unknown source in the Universe?

Are the ribbons cool, warm, wide, narrow, satin, grosgrain, velvet, or other fabrics or shapes?

Are they bright or soft colors, a variety of colors or only one color? Their softness cushions you.

They are dissolving into you, grounding, centering, and balancing. You feel peaceful and calm.

The ribbons are protective, gifts of courage, strength,

~ Finding Peace ~

laughter, friendship, hope, and anything else you ask of them. Does anything come to mind now?

Gently wrap your beautiful ribbons around the hurting world.

Accept and share your gifts of Grace, Light, Blessing, and Healing in any way you can, consciously, deliberately, with Intention, and without hesitation. When you are present and attentive in the company of others, you are sharing these gifts.

Offer thanks and close by taking relaxation breaths.

Somewhere someone needs help. Send love. It matters.
— Carrie Newcomer,
"Send Love, It Matters"

Julian's Prayer Meditation

This prayer has been attributed to Julian of Norwich (1343 – c. 1416), an English anchoress (hermit) of the Middle Ages. Her writings, now known as Revelations of Divine Love, are the earliest surviving English language works by a woman.

Intentions: To instill hope and light into your nervous system and all body cells. To be strengthened, grounded, and connected to heart, mind, and body.

Julian: "Await Spirit's Presence however it may come to you." Take a relaxation breath. Picture a bright white or deep indigo light at the top of your head at the Crown Chakra. Expand it into the center of the Universe. As it expands, it lifts your Soul Light along with it.

Julian: "Allow the Sense of Spirit's Presence to come or not and be what it is." Take a relaxation breath. Knowing that we are made of star stuff, scoop up a handful of the brightest star, Vega. Bring this Light down a star beam into your Crown Chakra and let it fill your head, neck, arms, the trunk of your body, and your legs until you are filled with starlight.

~ Finding Peace ~

Send the Light into Mother Earth through the soles/souls of your feet and ground yourself there. You are connected to the Universe and Earth.

Julian: "Accept as a Gift whatever comes or does not come. Accept that you don't know everything and that you are not in charge." Take a relaxation breath. If your Light diminishes and dims and hope seems to dim along with it, remember that you are not in charge. You do have a responsibility to care for yourself and others with whatever gifts you are given. Consider a way you can care for yourself. Consider a gift that only you may have and how you could use it.

Julian: "Attend to what you are called to. Be willing to be present and to be Spirit's love in the world however Spirit calls you to be." Take a relaxation breath. Open yourself at your Heart Center to any possible way you may be led to be Spirit's love in the world.

Because we are all connected, when we experience anything, we experience everything. When we hope for the common good, it will continue to grow in us and go into the collective hope of the Universe.

Give thanks for your gifts and blessings. End with relaxation breaths.

> *But if, on a clear and moonless night you stand*
> *on a hilltop away from the haze of civilization,*
> *where the dazzle of a billion, trillion heavenly bodies*
> *glitters the sky, settles around your shoulders,*
> *you will know in your heart, that no matter the strife,*
> *there will always be stars.*
>
> — Patricia Goodman
> "There Will Be Stars"

We Are All Healers Meditation

You may feel that the word healer is too powerful a word to define you, but we are all healers when we speak and act with kindness. We heal by using positive words, when we actively listen to family members, friends, and strangers, by putting an arm around someone we know well, laughing together, being patient, teaching, making donations of time and resources to organizations that help others, writing notes and cards, sending texts and emails, making a meal for someone in need, and in a myriad of other ways.

We heal ourselves by opening up to new ideas and people, being a quiet presence, meditating, praying, journaling, enjoying the arts, exercising, singing, dancing, reading, expressing gratitude, practicing a form of spirituality, and caring for our personal health. Healing is often done unconsciously, without thinking of it as such.

Intention: To consider your gifts of healing and ways you share them.

Serving – By what means do you serve others?

Teaching – How and whom do you teach?

Wisdom – You have matchless and invaluable knowledge. How do you use your Superpowers?

Giving – In what distinctive ways do you give of yourself to family, friends, to a group to which you belong, or to people whom you don't know? Do you donate to organizations that help those in need? If so, think of how your donation(s) may be helping others.

Creativity and Imagination – Consider how you are creative and imaginative. How do you utilize these unique gifts?

Being more conscious of your abilities as a healer may allow you to be more intentional in finding opportunities to utilize them.

Give and receive healing gifts graciously and with gratitude.

As you take relaxation breaths, give thanks for your gifts and talents.

You give but little when you give of your possessions.
It is when you give of yourself that you truly give.
— Kahlil Gibran

We are showered every day with gifts
but they are not meant for us to keep.
— Robin Wall Kimmerer
Braiding Sweetgrass

Gabriel, Strength of God Meditation

Archangel Gabriel is known as the Messenger of God. Archangels can be either gender or simply Light. Gabriel is often referred to as *she* because of her announcements of the births (female experiences) of John the Baptist to Zechariah and a son to Mary. Gabriel guided the Three Wise Men to the place where Jesus was born. For these reasons, she is sometimes thought of as the Christmas Angel. Gabriel is referenced in the Old Testament book of Enoch and in numerous ancient Hebrew writings. Islam regards Gabriel as an archangel sent by God to various prophets, including Muhammed, to whom he gave the Quran.

As you take relaxation breaths, breathe into a sense of calm. Ground yourself with the breath.

Intention: To be open to ways in which Gabriel can be of service to you.

Explore your beliefs about angels. Do they feel real to you? If so, how? If not, why?
Some of Gabriel's Gifts of Service:

Creative Projects – Are you working on a project where help would be appreciated?

~ Finding Peace ~

Transition – Are you in a period of transition? How could Gabriel help?

Forgiveness – If you need to let go of anger and offer forgiveness to someone, including yourself, speak to Gabriel about the situation and ways to do so.

Relationships – Gabriel can strengthen relationships, those already strong and those in need of repair. Reflect on the relationships in your life and how you can strengthen them.

Spiritual development and growth – Review your Spiritual beliefs and ask for deeper understanding and expansion. What are ways you can continue to grow?

Alignment – (physical, emotional, mental). How are you caring for yourself?

Finding Life's Purpose – (this may change as you go through life). What do you feel is your current life's purpose?

One of Archangel Gabriel's key messages and reminders is that we are all unique expressions of the Divine. Gabriel encourages living a life centered around love, compassion, gratitude, and kindness.

Set aside time each day to meditate, pray, journal, or simply sit in silence and invite Gabriel to make her presence known to you. Stay present, centered, grounded, and open to allow the subtle guidance, creative inspiration, and wisdom of Gabriel to appear. It will not be with words. Trust your intuition. Give thanks for your many blessings as you take relaxation breaths.

Adventure in Moving

When our children were young, we had an opportunity to move to Denver for ten months, from August to May. In one weekend, we left our children with family three hours away, flew to Denver where my husband was hired on the spot for a development job, rented a small carriage house, enrolled our daughter in second grade and flew back to Delaware where we lived. During the next two weeks we rented our home to a friend, stored almost all of our furniture in the basement, bought a station wagon, packed bare necessities into a U-Haul and hired two college students to drive it to Colorado, contracting to pay all expenses except speeding tickets. We then flew back to Colorado to start our adventure.

My husband's job entailed covering several nearby states. Our daughter was young enough to be taken out of school periodically for a week at a time and our son, three years younger, was in preschool half days a few days a week, so we were able to take many trips. It was wonderful to visit so much of the West, to make new friends and enjoy diverse experiences.

The February we lived in Denver my husband was offered a position as Director of Development for North America at a college in Lebanon. He accepted immediately despite the late May start date. In March a major airline offered a special for families which included the husband flying full price anywhere in the USA; wife, half price; and children flying free. Both of our fathers had coronaries during this time away, and we took advantage of the offer and flew east for a week to see both families, one in New Jersey and the other in Pennsylvania, three hours away from Delaware where we lived and where we were staying in a friend's home. We had been told of a house going on the market on a street we loved.

~ Finding Peace ~

We contacted the owners, whom we knew, and arranged to see it while back east. When we walked in the front door, I knew immediately that it would be our happiest family home, which it became for the next thirty-six years. We signed to buy it on the spot.

We purchased a Datsun in Colorado so I could ferry the children about while my husband travelled in the station wagon to outlying areas. When his Colorado job ended in early May, we began the journey home, having packed our belongings in a U-Haul attached to the station wagon, with me following in the Datsun. Because my husband was booked to fly to Lebanon to visit the college and meet colleagues, and we were scheduled to settle contracts on the home we owned and on the new home and move into it upon our arrival, our trip across country was not as leisurely as we had originally planned.

As I drove cross country behind the U-Haul for long hours daily, I was constantly aware of the "Adventure in Moving" motto painted on the back door of the U-Haul. Despite the challenges of the journey and mishaps delaying our return to Delaware, we appreciated the beauty of our country and the joy of traveling with our children on the way to our new home and, in some ways, our new lives.

I feel that the motto "Adventure in Moving" could be a metaphor for all our lives. We experience difficult challenges and mishaps, some of them painful and delaying, but there is also beauty, wonder, and joy as we journey from this life to our next home and adventure.

Afterword

Writing and publishing *Finding Peace* has been one of the most intense and exciting experiences of my life.

As I revised previously written stories, wrote meditations and additional essays, and compiled them into chakra categories, my energy practitioner and a first reader reminded me that the actual creative process falls into chakra categories as well, but in reverse order, top to bottom, Crown to Root.

Utilizing each chakra's traits, as I moved from one stage of writing through the next, was encouraging and supportive. My thoughts about how the chakras related to writing this book are mentioned below. The word Trust should be added to all the statements.

Crown – Opening myself to receive and accept Spiritual guidance and connection to my Higher Self to begin the project.

Brow (Third Eye) – Following my intuition that the book was needed and that I had the intellect and perceptual abilities to accomplish writing it.

Throat – Communicating my thoughts and ideas as truthfully, clearly, and peacefully as possible.

Heart – Sharing love and compassion willingly with readers.

Solar Plexus – Having the courage, confidence, determination, and strength to take the risk.

Sacral – Expecting and receiving the abundant joy and pleasure of creative expression.

~ Finding Peace ~

Root – Grounding and centering physically, emotionally, mentally, and spiritually while honoring my life force during the demanding writing process.

And finally, birthing the book!

Thank you for reading *Finding Peace*.

As in independent author, your thoughts about my book are important to me. If you enjoyed this book, please leave a review on your favorite website.

~ Thank you,
Judith (Judy) Stoddard

Glossary

Affirmations – The acts of stating something positively; help overcome self-doubt and negative thoughts. When repeated and *believed*, they can help make positive changes. Empirical studies show that self-affirmations may mitigate the effects of stress.

Biofield – The human energy field or aura; the subtle (unseen) energy surrounding the physical body as far out as we can reach with arms extended. The biofield is more diffuse than the physical body and is not visible but is considered part of the physical body. It radiates out about 5-8 feet horizontally and 2-3 feet above the head and below the feet. It is composed of both subtle energy (chi, ki prana) and electromagnetic energy (bioplasma, the magnetic fluid that surrounds all living things).

Centering – To be "at home" in oneself; coming into our core, the inner place where we quiet the mind and heart, going to our deep peace within; being aware of our energies; "being" rather than "doing."

Chakra – Sanskrit word meaning "spinning wheel"; vortex; human energy centers.

Chi/Qi (pronounced Chee) – Chinese word for energy or vital life force flowing through chakras, meridians, and biofield. Also called prana, ki, spiritus.

Complementary Therapy – Used with traditional medical interventions/treatments. Examples: energy modalities

~ Finding Peace ~

(Healing Touch, Reiki), Emotional Freedom Technique (EFT/tapping), massage, yoga, Qigong, Tai Chi, acupuncture and acupressure, kinesiology, etc.

Cortisol – The stress hormone; a glucocorticoid hormone produced and released by the adrenal glands that sit atop the kidneys; helps regulate the stress response, suppress inflammation, and control metabolism and sugar levels, among other benefits. Chronic high levels due to prolonged stress can have negative health effects. Cortisol levels may be reduced by meditation and other mindfulness activities.

Creative Visualization – A cognitive process of forming clear mental images through the imagination with the intention of manifesting goals or positive outcomes; usually paired with meditation and mindfulness.

Cure – To relieve a person of the symptoms of a disease or condition.

Energetic Cord – An invisible thread connecting individuals; a spiritual "rope" that attaches one person's lifeforce or aura to another person's life force or aura. People are born with some of these cords and attach others throughout life.

Energetic Sweeping – Physical (using hands) or mental sweeping to release and remove toxins, strengthen the immune system, and clear the body and energetic field of congested or stagnant energy.

Grace – The kindness given to us by Spirit: Prayer, thanksgiving, and blessing. Synonyms: benevolence, favor, goodness, goodwill, elegance, poise, ease, refinement, gracefulness.

Gratitude – The emotional state of being thankful; readiness to show appreciation for and return kindness; an affirmation of goodness and warmth.

Grounding – Connecting to the Earth and Earth's energy field to calm the mind and balance the entire energy system.

Heal – To be made whole. Often mistakenly interchanged with the word cure.

Healing Touch – A centuries-old holistic energy therapy in which practitioners use their hands in a heart-centered and intentional way to support, balance, and facilitate physical, emotional, mental, and spiritual health; promotes relaxation and supports healing by decreasing anxiety, stress, and tension and enhancing well-being; a nontoxic, non-invasive, effective, and economical healing modality.

Highest Good – If used in spiritual context: what keeps a person on a path toward their soul's purpose, the ultimate reason why someone is here on earth. Life led in communion with Spirit.

Higher Power – Spiritual belief or connection greater than ourselves that offers a sense of love, peace, caring, purpose, and inner strength. Descriptive names: Spirit, God, Goddess, Holy/Great Spirit, Divine, Source, Yahweh, Allah, Lord, Deity, etc.

Holistic – Relates to the whole person: physical, emotional, mental, and spiritual, which represent the matrix of the biofield.

Intention (as related to the meditations in this book) – Placing oneself in Spirit's hands; requesting specific guidance, help, and direction during the meditation; utilizing the Law of Attraction.

Law of Attraction – Like Attracts Like; positive thoughts manifest positive results while negative thoughts manifest negative outcomes.

Light – Physical light, a natural phenomenon seen by the eyes; Spiritual Light, an inner guiding or enlightening force or power; something divine in the human soul; Infinite Light seen as a type of divine energy that exists outside of time and space.

Liminal – Adjective: relating to a threshold or border between two things, states, or conditions; derived from the Latin word "limen," which means "threshold."

Liminal Space – The transitional space or time in which one phase shifts to another; neither in the previous phase nor in the next one; the middle ground between two grounds.

Meditation – Reflective thinking or contemplation. The most common types include mindfulness, visualization, intentional breathing, sitting or lying quietly, spiritual practices such as prayer, intentional movement, mandalas, and chanting among many others. All require different skill sets.

Meditation Positions – Sitting, standing, kneeling, lying down, moving (Qi Gong; walking, etc.). Seated meditation position: sit with spine straight, feet flat on the floor, shoulders, neck, and facial muscles relaxed, hands resting gently in lap or on thighs. Tilting the elbows slightly outward helps to help open the chest for improved breathing.

Meridians – Traditional Chinese Medicine (TCM) energy flow lines coursing through the physical body that are studied and manipulated to promote healing in acupuncture and acupressure treatment. *Yin* (female) energy moves upward; *yang* (male) energy, downward. They are utilized in energy modalities.

Relaxation Breaths – Mindful technique to help illicit the body's relaxation response, characterized by slower breathing, lowered blood pressure and heart rate. Deep inhalation through the nose. Exhalation through the mouth is usually twice as long; a grounding and centering technique.

Spiritual – As differentiated from any specific religious belief or practice; each person's unique connection to some power greater than their personal self. Practices to enhance spiritual awareness may include being still, meditating, praying, breathing purposefully, grounding to the Earth, setting Intention, journaling, crafting, creating, listening carefully, and learning to trust intuition.

Subtle Energy Body – The biofield, chakras, meridians, and auras.

Synchronicity – A word used by psychiatrist Carl Jung to describe simultaneous coincidental events, especially psychic events, which may appear related but have no discernable causal connection. Synchronicity events may feel meaningful and significant and provide guidance.

Thin Places – A term originating from Celtic spirituality referring to places or experiences where separation between heaven and earth is narrowed (thin); allows encounters with Spirit's presence more directly.

Universe – Thirteen point eight billion years old; encompasses everything that exists: matter and energy, including physical laws that influence them; all of space/cosmos and the world of human experience. There is a concept called *Multiverse,* suggesting other universes may exist beyond our observable universe.

Universal Energy Field – A concept in quantum physics proven by Nobel Prize-winning physicists that everything in the Universe is made up of energy that flows and constantly changes form, including humans.

Bibliography

Alcantara, Margarita. *Chakra Healing, A Beginners Guide to Self-Healing Techniques That Balance the Chakras.* Embassy Books, Mumbai, India, 2021

Andrews, Ted. *Animal Speak, The Spiritual & Magical Powers of Creatures Great & Small,* Llewellyn Worldwide; Woodbury, MN, 2007

Angelou, Maya. *Amazing Peace*; A Celebration. Random House, New York, NY, 2005

Borysenko, Joan, PH.D. *Pocketful of Miracles, Prayers, Meditations and Affirmations.* Warner Books, New York, NY, 1994

Brach, Tara. *Trusting the Gold, Uncovering Your Natural Goodness.* Sounds True Publishing, Louisville, CO, 80027, 2021

Butje, Andrea. *The Heart of Aromatherapy, An Easy to Use Guide for Essential Oils.* Black and Butje, Inc., Saint Petersburg, FL, 2022

Cameron, Julia. *The Artist's Way, A Spiritual Guide to Higher Creativity.* TarcherPerigree, New York, NY, 30th Edition, 2016

Dyer, Dr.Wayne W. *The Power of Intention; Learning to Co-Create Your World Your Way.* Hayhouse, USA, 2009

Emmons, PHD, Robert A. *Thanks! How Practicing Gratitude Can Make You Happier,* Harper One Group, San Francisco, CA., 2008

Gerber, MD, Richard. *Vibrational Medicine, The #1 Handbook of Subtle-Energy Therapies.* Bear and Company, Rochester, VT, 2001

Goldberg, Natalie. *Writing Down the Bones, Freeing the Writer Within.* Shambhala, Boston, MA, 30th Anniversary Edition 2016

Goldberg, Natalie. *Old Friend from Far Away, The Practice of Writing Memoir.* Free Press (Simon & Schuster, New York, NY, 2008

Hay, Louise L. *Heal Your Body, The Mental Causes for Physical Illness and the Metaphysical Way to Overcome Them.* Hay House Publishing, Inc., Carlsbad, CA, 1988

Hover-Kramer, Dorothea. *Healing Touch Guidebook, Practicing the Art and Science of Human Caring.* Twentieth Anniversary Edition, Healing Touch Program Publisher, San Antonia, TX, 2009

Judith, Anodea. *Wheels of Life, A User's Guide to the Chakra System.* Llewellyn Worldwide (formerly Llewellyn Publisher), Woodbury, MN, 1987

Kabat-Zinn, Jon. *Wherever You Go, There You Are, Mindfulness Meditation in Everyday Life.* Hatchette Book Group, New York, NY, 30th Anniversary Edition, 2023

Kimmerer, Robin Walls. *Braiding Sweetgrass, Indigenous Wisdom, Scientific Knowledge, and the Teachings of Plants.* Milkweed Editions, Canada, 2013

Lamott, Anne. *Help, Thanks, Wow, the Three Essential Prayers.* Penguin Group, New York, NY, 2012

Lamott, Anne. *Traveling Mercies, Some Thoughts on Faith.* Anchor Publishing, Alaska, 2000

Maue, Carolyn. *Gourmet Leadership, Turn up the heat on your secret sauce!.* Gravitas Press, United States, 2022

Myss, Carolyn. *Anatomy of the Spirit, The Seven Stages of Power and Healing.* Bantam Books (Transworld Publishers division of Random House Group), New York, NY, 1997

Myss, Carolyn. *Sacred Contracts, Awakening Your Divine Potential.* Sounds True Publishing, Louisville, CO, 2002

Newell, J. Phillip. *Listening for the Heartbeat of God, A Celtic Spirituality*. SPCK Publishing, UK, 2008

Nhat Hanh, Thich. *The Miracle of Mindfulness, An Introduction to the Practice of Meditation*. Beacon Press, Boston, MA, 1999

O'Donohue, John. *Anam Cara, A Book of Celtic Wisdom*. HarperCollins, New York, NY, 2004

O'Donohue, John. *To Bless the Space Between Us, A Book of Blessings*. Penguin Random House LLC, New York, NY, 2008

Oschman, James L. *Energy Medicine, The Scientific Basis*. Churchill Livingstone and Imprint of Elsevier, Philadelphia, PA, 2nd Edition, 2015

Sanders, Pete. A. Jr. *You Are Psychic! The Free Soul Method*. Fireside Publishing, New York, NY, 2016

Tolle, Eckhardt. *The Power of Now, A Guide to Spiritual Enlightenment*. New World Library, Canada, 2004

Worwood, Valerie Ann. *The Complete Book of Essential Oils and Aromatherapy*; New World Library, Novato, CA 2016

Children's Books

Keleny, Christine. *Chakra Magic* (ages 3 to 12 years), CKBooks Publishing, New Glarus, WI, 2018

Ortner, Alex. *Gorilla Thumps & Bear Hugs: A Tapping Solution Children's Story*. Hay House, New York, NY, 2016

Van der Meer, Maya. Kuan Yin, *The Princes Who Became the Goddess of Compassion*. Shambhala Publications, Inc., Boulder, CO, 2021

Resources

Abebooks.com – Web site to purchase inexpensive, secondhand books in good condition.

Association for Comprehensive Energy Psychology (ACEP) (energypsych.org); Information regarding evidenced based methods that influence the human bio-energy systems such as meridians, chakras, and the biofield to promote holistic wellbeing.

Balance Through Simplicity – (https://balancethrough-simplicity.com/), A blog and free resources dedicated to helping declutter your home, simplify life, and live intentionally.

Chakra Tune Up with Himalayan Singing Bowls (11 Minutes) https://www.youtube.com/watch?v=-ar9vsmFhJU

Cleveland Clinic – (Clevelandclinic.org); Health topics resource.

Dailyom.com – Nonsectarian inspirational essays, poems, and thoughts.

Emotional Freedom Technique (EFT). Tapping 101 (thetappingsolution.com); Site to learn the basics of the Tapping Technique.

Energy Magazine (energymagazineonline.com); Holistic health and energy medicine articles.

Gratefulness.org – Short daily gratefulness quotes by well-known authors.

Harvard Health Publishing (https://www.health.harvard.edu/); Health topics resource.

Healing Beyond Borders (www.healingbeyondborders.org) and Healing Touch Program (http://healingtouchprogram.com/), Sites for information about Healing Touch classes.

InsightTimer.com – Excellent source for free meditations.

Mayo Clinic – (mayoclinic.org); Health topics resource.

National Institute of Health (nih.gov.com); Official website of the National Institutes of Health (NIH), one of the world's foremost medical research centers. NIH is the agency of the U.S. Department of Health and Human Services.

Psychology Today – (http://psychologytoday.com); Articles on behavioral research and practical guidance on mental health and wellbeing subjects.

Qi Gong; Lee Holden – (https://www.youtube.com/watch?v=pj4qo2KL9f4); 20 Minute Morning Qi Gong Exercises for beginners.

University of Pennsylvania Health System Penn Medicine (www.pennmedicine.org); Health topics resources.

Soundstrue.com-Site that partners with spiritual teachers making their teachings accessible on multimedia platforms.

The Johns Hopkins Hospital (www.hopkinsmedicine.org); Health topics resources.

DVDs or Live Streaming:
  Netflix:
Fantastic Fungi – Underground network that help trees communicate, Louie Schwartzberg, Director.

Amazon Prime Video:
Death Makes LIFE Possible – Transforming the Fear of Death into an Inspiration for Living and Dying Well (8 Awards).

Heal – Change Your Mind, Change Your Body, Change Your Life; Stars Dr. Deepak Chopra, Dr. Joe Dispenza, Anita Moorjani, et al. Directed by Kelly Noonan Gores and Adam Schomer.

The Living Matrix – A film on the new science of healing.

Images
(in order of appearance)

Pg 11, Peter Hermes Furian – Shutterstock
Pg 13, AndyKali – Wikipedia
Pg 14, chakra – anatomy.com
Pg 15, irongroup – Pixabay
Pg 17, Joe-jplenio – Pixabay
Pg 20, Hans – Pixabay
Pg 22, Jurgen – Pixabay
Pg 26, Jill Wellington – Pixabay
Pg 32, u11116-Margo Lipa - Pixabay
Pg 36, Yuri – Pixabay
Pg 39, #1828012 – Pixabay
Pg 43, Mirzolotz – Wikipedia
Pg 44, crystalvaults.com/sacral-chakra-explained
Pg 45, piselperfectmom – Pixabay
Pg 48, Claudia Berbeo – Pixabay
Pg 52, Daniel Roberts – Pixabay
Pg 60, americanmeadow.com
Pg 65, AndyKali and Ista Derata – Wikipedia
Pg 66, paulcheksblog.com/the-chakra-system-part-3-the-solar-plexus-chakra/
Pg 70, Matthias – Pixabay
Pg 73, Gunter/Moritz320 – Pixabay
Pg 76, Hans – Pixabay
Pg 78, Pepril-Petr Preucil – Pixabay
Pg 85, Jill Wellington – Pixabay
Pg 87, Asvsgr – Pixabay
Pg 91, Atarax42 – Wikipedia
Pg 92, japamalabeads.com

Pg 93, Huems – Pixabay
Pg 99, Freepik #34136582
Pg 104, Tamalele/Peter H – Pixabay
Pg 106, aminaria-vest – Pixabay
Pg 108, Nowaja – Pixabay
Pg 112, Annette Meyer – Pixabay
Pg 121, Atarx42 – Wikipedia
Pg 122, crystalvaults.com/throat-chakra-explained
Pg 123, andrewsbird – Pixabay
Pg 128, LeQuocHuy36 - Pixabay
Pg 134, FerraraMedia – Pixabay
Pg 137, Atarax4 – Wikipedia
Pg 138, crystalvaults.com/brow-chakra-explained
Pg 139, drquanli – Pixabay
Pg 144, Gerd Altmann – Pixabay
Pg 148, Michael Schwarzen – Pixabay
Pg 151, Meredin – Pixabay
Pg 155, chakra-anatomy.com
Pg 156, midtownyogastudios.com/blog/crown-chakra
Pg 159, Submeet – Pixabay
Pg 161, Gerd Altmann – Pixabay
Pg 163, Gerd Altmann – Pixabay
Pg 165, Robyn Mackenzie – Shutterstock
Pg 167, Kerstin Riemer – Pixabay

Acknowledgments

The help and support I received while writing and birthing *Finding Peace* was extensive. My thanks to everyone who participated.

My four first readers brought their considerable skills to the early draft, and their insights and comments were valuable and encouraging.

Kathleen McKenzie's enthusiasm as I began the book was heartening. She helped refine chakra characteristics and made suggestions for placement of specific meditations and stories. Kathleen has kept me in balance energetically for years.

Regina Pippidis, soul sister and friend, is the most thoughtful and attentive listener I have ever known. Her intuitive reflections and related questions helped to clarify my thinking. We attended the first four levels of the Healing Touch course together, and this gave her a unique understanding of my work.

Carol Hogue, a member of the Women's Holistic Spiritual Retreat Planning Committee, made suggestions for standardization of format and understood the *why* and *what* of the book. Carol was immediately on board as a reader when I asked, "Would you consider. . . ?"

Maria Pippidis willingly offered her assistance and spent a significant amount of time carefully reviewing the draft and posing important questions about intent and objectives for me to consider.

Carolyn Maue, lifelong friend and author of *Gourmet Leadership, Turn up the heat on your secret sauce!* freely shared her experience with writing and publishing and gave help and support at critical junctures. Carolyn and I always laugh together.

Participants in the Women's Holistic Spiritual Retreat became the Core Retreaters Zoom group, morphing into an important, steadfast, and dependable group of supporters.

The Friends and Friends of Friends Meditation Zoom group brings me joy. Although many members have not met, all express feelings of care and concern for one another and have given uplifting feedback following the meditations.

Jon Harrison, editor par excellence, was straightforward, knowledgeable, and meticulous. I learned a considerable amount working with Jon and appreciated his expertise. I am grateful to have found him via the Editorial Freelancers Association (EFA).

Christine Keleny, CKBooks Publishing, was instrumental in helping turn my vision into reality. She is creative, experienced, helpful, patient, and a pleasure to work with. Christine was highly recommended to me and using her as publisher was an excellent choice.

Family and friends have expressed excitement and enthusiasm about my writing *Finding Peace* while remaining somewhat mystified about what it was I was writing.

My husband, Bob, author of *Sarah and Her Sisters, American Missionary Pioneers in Arab Female Education, 1834-1937*, made excellent suggestions on how to simplify my stories and other writing, making them more readable. I am beyond appreciative of his patience in frequently having meals served at a late hour and for his periodically taking on household responsibilities so I could continue to write, often interrupting his own writing to do so. Bob's support and love are beyond measure.

Sincere and heartfelt thanks not only to everyone mentioned above but also to all of you, the readers of *Finding Peace*.

Judith Lynch Stoddard

About the Author

Judy Stoddard, RN, BS ED, CHTP is a certified Healing Touch Practitioner, experienced nurse, and teacher. She is a graduate of Polyclinic Hospital School of Nursing and Temple University. Judy has been practicing Healing Touch since July 2006 following a traditional career in nursing.

She taught student nurses at Thomas Jefferson University Hospital and classes in Preparation for Childbirth at the former Wilmington General Hospital (now Christiana Care Health System). She later worked for Planned Parenthood of Delaware and as a College Health Nurse at Widener University, Delaware Campus, and at Delaware Technical and Community College, Stanton Campus. During this time, she earned a certification in College Health Nursing by The American Nurses Credentialing Center. Judy's job for the Delaware Chapter of the Leukemia and Lymphoma Society was Patient Services Manager where she received the Superior Achievement Award. She was a volunteer at Delaware Hospice, Nemours Hospital for Children, Delaware, ReadAloud Delaware, and mentored at Highlands Elementary School. Judy also did clowning for ten years while working part time.

Judy has been interested in integrative medical practices her entire nursing career, which led her to study Healing Touch. Judy is certified as a Healing Touch Practitioner by Healing Beyond Borders (formerly Healing Touch International) and is a member of that organization. She has had six essays published in Healing Beyond Border's "Perspectives in Healing" quarterly e-newsletter. Her contribution on holistic end of life care with a client was published in the *Healing*

~ Finding Peace ~

Touch Guidebook, 20th Anniversary Edition by Dorothea Hover-Kramer (2009).

Judy meditates and walks daily, is an avid reader, loves to travel, journals semi-frequently, and leads two online women's zoom groups. Family gatherings head the list of favorite things.

You can connect with Judith online at facebook.com/judith.stoddard.9.

∽

If you enjoyed this book, please leave a review at your favorite book websites online. This is very helpful to an indie-author like Judith.

Thank you!

www.ingramcontent.com/pod-product-compliance
Lightning Source LLC
Chambersburg PA
CBHW071917290426
44110CB00013B/1394